SENSIBLE
MATHEMATICS
SECOND EDITION

A Guide for **School Leaders** in the Era
of Common Core State Standards

STEVEN LEINWAND

HEINEMANN
Portsmouth, NH

Heinemann
361 Hanover Street
Portsmouth, NH 03801–3912
www.heinemann.com

Offices and agents throughout the world

The author and publisher wish to thank those who have generously given permission to reprint borrowed material:

"Cholesterol Pill May Help the Healthy" by Rita Rubin from *USA TODAY,* May 27, 1998. Copyright © 1998 by USA TODAY, a division of Gannett Co., Inc. Reprinted by permission of the publisher.

Table entitled "Teens' Tobacco Choices" from "Tobacco Bill Not Equal for All Products" by Wendy Koch from *USA TODAY,* May 27, 1998. Copyright © 1998 by USA TODAY, a division of Gannett, Co., Inc. Reprinted by permission of the publisher.

"Faulty Bridge Sign Traps Truck" by Robyn Adams from *Waterbury Republican-American*, January 25, 1995. Copyright © 1995 by Waterbury Republican-American. Reprinted by permission of the publisher.

"Television Viewing Habits and Their Impact," from *A Guide to K-12 Program Development in Mathematics.* Copyright © 1999 by the Connecticut State Board of Education. Reprinted with permission.

(credits continue on page iv)

Library of Congress Cataloging-in-Publication Data
Leinwand, Steve.
  Sensible mathematics : a guide for school leaders in the era of common core state standards / Steven Leinwand. — 2nd ed.
      p. cm.
  Includes bibliographical references.
  ISBN-13: 978-0-325-04382-1
  ISBN-10: 0-325-04382-5
  1. Mathematics—Study and teaching. 2. Curriculum planning. I. Title.
  QA11.L45 2012
  510.71'2—dc23   2012003981

Editor: Katherine S. Bryant
Production editor: Sonja S. Chapman
Typesetter: Shawn Girsberger
Cover design: George Kokkonas
Interior design: Monica Ann Crigler
Manufacturing: Steve Bernier

Printed in the United States of America on acid-free paper
16   15   14   13   12   ML   1   2   3   4   5

To Ann,
as always
∞

CONTENTS

Introduction
Change Requires Leadership

Changing people's behavior is one of the most difficult aspects of leadership. However, there is much that we know about changing behaviors:

- people cannot do what they cannot *envision*;
- people will not do what they do not *believe* is possible;
- people will not implement what they do not *understand*;
- people are unlikely to do well what they don't *practice*;
- people who practice without *feedback* don't progress efficiently; and
- people who work without *collaboration* are unlikely to sustain their effort.

The combination of these simple truisms leads us to the heart of providing effective leadership for school mathematics programs: Leaders must help people envision, believe, understand, practice, receive feedback, and work collaboratively!

And why is change in K–12 school mathematics so urgent? First, we are being asked to shift *from* a mathematics program that, based on the number of students currently deemed proficient, rarely works for more than 40 percent of the student population *to* a program that empowers nearly all students. There is no road map or existence proof that such a shift can be made, but that is exactly what schools are being asked to do. Second, we are being asked to shift *from* a program that has focused primarily on computational skills and symbol manipulation (e.g., factoring and simplifying) *to* a program that builds deep understanding of key mathematical ideas and promotes application of skills and concepts. Anything less ignores the impact of technology and the demands of today's workplace. Third, we are being asked to shift *from* a dominant instructional model of teaching by showing and telling *to* a model of orchestrating learning through engaging tasks and having students grapple with mathematical ideas. In other words, we are being asked to teach in distinctively different ways from how nearly all current teachers were taught—a challenge for which there are few existence proofs. And all three of these shifts are being expected as part of the brave new world represented by the Common Core State Standards for Mathematics (CCSSM). Without strong, clear, and effective forms of leadership, it is unlikely that these critical shifts can be realized.

This book provides ideas and insights into what teacher leaders, mathematics coaches, department heads, math supervisors, and school and district administrators need to know and do to implement high-quality K–12 mathematics that provide opportunities for all students to learn mathematics. More specifically, this book attempts to meet the need for broader understanding, clearer perspective, and effective and easy-to-use tools by serving as a mathematics improvement guidebook for school leaders. As a toolkit, this book provides principals and other school leaders with a broad array of strategies, a diverse arsenal of ammunition, and several "how-to" game plans for providing leadership for the substantial improvement of kindergarten through twelfth-grade mathematics programs. It is designed to provide reasonable and cogent answers to many of the issues that educators face when they are called upon to deal with a school's or district's mathematics program. And it is written to help assure that all of America's mathematics classrooms better meet the higher expectations that result from changing societal and economic forces at work in every corner of our economy and our society.

In the ten or so years since the first edition of *Sensible Mathematics* was published, I have continued to be blessed with the opportunity to learn and grow while working in diverse schools and districts across the country. It has been extraordinarily rewarding to see many of the ideas presented in the book being productively implemented in ways that truly serve teachers and students. It has also been very frustrating to see how slow the process of change can be, how resistant to change the system can be, and how much still needs to be done to provide *all* students with viable opportunities to learn mathematics. This second edition of *Sensible Mathematics* retains those parts of the first edition that still capture what math leaders need to know and do. It also expands to draw on what I've learned over these past ten years and addresses what I believe are new challenges and opportunities represented by the era of the Common Core State Standards for Mathematics.

What has been most amazing is how much has changed during a decade that began with No Child Left Behind and has been marked by unrelenting pressure to raise test scores, and ended with the vision and hope of the Common Core State Standards for Mathematics and a long-overdue recognition that it's the quality of daily instruction that matters most. However, what has *not* changed much at all is the overall quality of that classroom instruction or the support that teachers need in order to significantly raise the effectiveness of instructional practice. As has always been the case, achieving this level of quality and support requires school leaders who can help the people they work with to change their beliefs and biases, their perspectives and understandings, and ultimately their behaviors, all in pursuit of higher levels of mathematics achievement by greater numbers of students.

Providing effective leadership is never easy. Providing effective leadership for school mathematics programs in an era of unprecedented pressure to raise mathematics achievement and expectations for broad implementation of the ambitious Common Core State Standards for Mathematics is particularly challenging. This book is designed to help school leaders meet these challenges.

1

The Math Leader's Domains of Responsibility

School principals and other school leaders face enormous challenges in the realm of elementary, middle, and high school mathematics. The issues teachers face today in providing high-quality mathematics programs are not trivial. Resolving these issues in ways that best serve the young people in our schools is not easy. Balancing the often competing interests and positions of students, teachers, policy makers, and parents in the face of single-minded pressures for higher levels of achievement and narrowing achievement gaps is difficult. And maintaining focus on what is best for students amid the tensions that abound when people are being asked to change what they do and how they do it is incredibly hard to accomplish.

But just as teachers help students learn best when they reduce confusion and define what a student doesn't understand, we too can delimit the field of responsibility for leaders into the four core components of K–12 mathematics programs at the heart of ensuring program quality and producing high levels of student achievement:

- a coherent and aligned **curriculum** that includes a set of grade-level content expectations, appropriate print and electronic instructional materials, and a pacing guide that links the content standards, the materials, and the calendar;

- high levels of **instructional effectiveness**, guided by a shared vision of teaching and learning mathematics, and supported by deliberate planning, attention to, and reflection about the details of effective practice;

- a set of aligned benchmark and summative **assessments** that allow for monitoring of student, teacher, and school accomplishment at the unit/chapter and grade/course levels; and

- **professional growth** within a **professional culture** of dignity, transparency, collaboration, and support.

These are the "what," the "how," the "how well," and the "how supported and sustained" that constitute the four key interconnected components of a mathematics program. Figure 1–1 graphically displays these four components. Let's take a quick look at each of these components in the era of the Common Core State Standards.

Figure 1–1   *The four core components of a mathematics program*

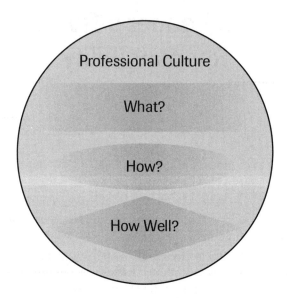

THE CURRICULUM

For as long as most of us can remember, the K–12 mathematics program in the United States has been aptly characterized in many rather uncomplimentary ways: underperforming, incoherent, fragmented, poorly aligned, unteachable, unfair, narrow in focus, skill-based, and, of course, "a mile wide and an inch deep." Most teachers are well aware that there have been far too many objectives for each grade or course, few of them rigorous or conceptually oriented, and too many of them misplaced as we prematurely ram far too much computation down too many throats. It's certainly not a very pretty picture, and it helps to explain why so many teachers and students have been set up to fail and how we've created the need for much of the intervention that test results seem to require.

But hope and change have arrived! Like the long awaited cavalry, the new Common Core State Standards for Mathematics (CCSSM) presents us with a once in a lifetime opportunity to rescue ourselves and our students from the myriad curriculum problems we've faced for years. First, these new standards are *common*. No longer will publishers cater to a few large states and stuff their books with the union of fifty-one sets of demands. No longer will our assessments be developed by the lowest bidder and overwhelmingly made up of low-level multiple-choice items. Instead, the prospects of a *Common* Core set of standards are far shorter, more web-based, better focused instructional materials and computer-adaptive, computer-delivered, instantaneously scorable, constructed-response item assessments. It almost sounds too good to be true, but once everyone is pushing and pulling and lifting in the same direction, market forces and public and private investments will be all the incentive needed to ensure an aligned system of materials and assessments that support the implementation of the new standards.

But it is the quality of the standards themselves—particularly for grades K–8—that are the cause for such optimism. They are *coherent*. These standards replace the vagueness of strands (number, measurement, geometry, data, and algebra) with domains, clusters, and well-conceived progressions of standards. They are *fair*. Many procedures that we have been asked to teach at grade x, have been moved to grade $x + 1$, giving us all a chance to build prerequisite knowledge and slow down what has become a drag race through the curriculum. And they are *teachable*. There are only about thirty to forty standards, of varying sizes and depth, at each grade level, resulting in a far more manageable teaching load than the forty to sixty objectives per year that many of us now face.

Just as important as the content standards and paralleling the National Council of Teachers of Mathematics (NCTM) process standards, the eight standards for mathematical practice "describe varieties of expertise that mathematics educators at all levels should seek to develop in their students." Among these overarching practices that should guide planning, teaching, and assessing mathematics at all levels are making sense of and persevering in solving problems, reasoning abstractly and quantitatively, constructing viable arguments, and modeling with mathematics—key elements that distinguish mathematics from other disciplines.

It is fair to argue that the Common Core State Standards for Mathematics' most impressive contribution is that they have essentially ended the "math wars" that have plagued school mathematics for much of the twenty years since the 1989 release of the NCTM Curriculum and Evaluation Standards. All sides appear to have finally come together and compromised around the Common Core and buried long-wielded hatchets. In light of this long-overdue agreement about the essential content and this significant shift in the playing field, every school leader needs to understand the meaning and the implications of these new standards and be able to support their implementation. The fact that, for the first time, the United States has what is essentially a national curriculum, equivalent in quality to what is found in the highest scoring countries in the world, means that the focus of leadership can finally shift from arguing about *what math to teach* to *how best to teach* the agreed-upon content to all students.

INSTRUCTIONAL EFFECTIVENESS

While an effective and coherent mathematics program should be *guided* by a clear set of content standards, it must be *grounded* in a clear and shared vision of teaching and learning—the two critical reciprocal actions that link teachers and students and largely determine educational success. While curriculum, materials, professional development, assessment, and cultivating broad programmatic support are all necessary components of the educational enterprise, they have little real impact unless they are effectively enacted in each and every classroom where learning is facilitated, supported, and maximized.

There is much that we know about what students typically do in mathematics classes and how we need to respond.

- Students often forget—so we need to do more deliberate review.
- Students often see the mathematics differently—so we need to accommodate multiple representations.
- Students often approach the mathematics differently—so we need to value and celebrate alternative approaches to the math and different learning styles.
- Students often give unreasonable or ridiculous answers—so we need to focus on number sense and estimation.
- Students often don't understand the vocabulary—so we need to build language-rich classrooms.
- Students often ask, "Why do we need to know this?"—so we need to embed the content in relevant and authentic contexts.

In light of these daily classroom experiences, the good news is that research, classroom observations, and common sense provide a great deal of guidance about instructional practices that make significant differences in student achievement. These practices can be found in high-performing classrooms and schools at all levels and in all regions of the country. Effective teachers make the question "Why?" a classroom mantra to support a culture of reasoning and justification. Teachers incorporate daily, cumulative review of skills and concepts and formative assessment practices into instruction. Lessons are deliberately planned and skillfully employ alternative approaches and multiple representations—including pictures and concrete materials—as part of explanations and answers. Teachers rely on relevant contexts to engage their students' interest and use thought-provoking questions to stimulate their thinking and create language-rich mathematics classrooms.

In light of these research-affirmed practices for ensuring high levels of opportunity to learn, every school leader needs to understand these practices, recognize when they are occurring and when they aren't, and help to support their consistent and widespread implementation.

ASSESSMENTS

But the glue that holds a program together is the assessments we use to monitor quality, progress, and achievement. Our assessments tell us what is truly valued, they operationalize the content standards so we are clear on what they mean, and they drive our decisions about what and how we teach. When the primary mode of assessment is multiple-choice measures of skill, it should be no surprise that the primary focus of instruction is how to get right answers. That is why when the history of the No Child Left Behind era is written, it is likely that the positive aspects of disaggregating data and of ratcheting up accountability will be overshadowed by the negative aspects of narrowing the focus of most high-stakes tests to an assessment of skills at the expense of conceptual understanding, communicating mathematically, and solving complex problems.

On the other hand, when a mathematics program is assessed with a balanced array of formative assessment practices, common and aligned benchmark tests, and chapter/unit and summative assessments that measure the broad spectrum of expectations and provide timely, detailed reporting mechanisms, these powerful assessments can guide all aspects of the program in positive directions. This is the current hope of the important shift in how we do business from a series of fifty-one state assessments of marginal quality to a new generation of much higher-quality assessments from the Partnership for Assessments of College and Career Readiness (PARCC) and the Smarter Balanced Assessment Consortium (SBAC), beginning in the 2014–15 school year. It really is a new frontier with very bright possibilities for mathematics teaching and learning in the United States.

In light of these significant changes in what will be assessed and how it will be assessed, every school leader needs to understand the implications of these new forms of assessment and be prepared to make effective use of the avalanche of data that will soon emerge from these tools.

PROFESSIONAL GROWTH AND CULTURE

As important as they are as components of a program, neither standards nor assessments actually teach. The new Common Core State Standards for Mathematics and the emerging PARCC and SBAC common assessments are critically important components of improvement and indispensible pieces of a more coherent, focused, and aligned K–12 mathematics program. But standards don't teach—teachers teach. High-quality assessments help us focus and monitor, but instruction, not summative assessments, engenders learning. Tragically, at exactly the same time that support for teachers is most needed to ensure effective implementation of the Common Core State Standards, budget cuts have reduced the number of math coaches and resource teachers.

This is why two schools with the same curriculum, the same assessments, and essentially the same demographics can have such different student outcomes. In one school teachers are unobserved, undersupported, and isolated from one another's practices, with few opportunities or mechanisms to share and grow collaboratively. In the other school one finds regular classroom observations by colleagues, a slew of sharing and professional learning community activities, and an overwhelming spirit of "we're in this together." One school has a professional culture that demoralizes and stymies growth and improvement; the other has a culture of mutual respect, trust, and collaboration that energizes the work and processes high levels of student achievement.

In light of this need for much greater professional knowledge and collaboration, particularly as we shift toward the Common Core State Standards for Mathematics, every school leader needs to be able to support a positive and productive professional culture that is characterized by mutual respect, transparency, and collaboration.

COMMON QUESTIONS

Consider just a few of the troubling questions that principals and other school leaders are being asked to deal with.

- How do I win over legitimately jaded educators who assume that this round of change is just another fad that can be ignored, smugly assured that "this too will soon pass"?

- How much pencil-and-paper computation and symbol manipulation should still be taught to best prepare students for a world in which calculators and computers do computation far more quickly and accurately?

- How do we transform mathematics programs that have traditionally sorted out students with ruthless efficiency into programs that truly empower all students?

- How can we much more effectively differentiate instruction in order to be more successful with a much higher proportion of the student body, and specifically, what can we do to ensure interventions that truly narrow gaps?

- How do we convince parents that the mathematics that "worked so well for me" is not the mathematics that best serves their children and that their children are not, once again, being used as "guinea pigs"?

- How do we support teachers who, having been positively appraised and rewarded for using traditional "teaching by telling" approaches, now must shift instructional practices to meet higher and different expectations?

Enter the leader. Whether a building principal, curriculum director, mathematics program supervisor, math coach, or department head, someone needs to have reasonable answers to these and other questions or, as has happened in many communities, mathematics reform efforts get undermined, sidetracked, or abandoned completely.

On the surface, this seems to be a reasonable agenda. Yet in classrooms across America, teachers and administrators are asking "Why bother?" "How is it different this time?" "Why should we pay attention to these standards, both old and new?" "Why bother putting the time and effort into changing what I do, especially when it's so likely to be criticized and questioned?" "Why should I make changes that are almost assuredly going to make my life harder?" The simple fact is that the changes being advocated *do* make people's lives harder. As educators, we are being asked to do things differently, to do more, and to be more productive, often with no more time, no more training, and no greater resources.

Once again, enter the leader. Principals and other school leaders must be able to confidently and knowledgeably respond to these questions with helpful answers and useful guidance. In the absence of cogent answers to these "why bother" questions and tangible support for those willing to take risks, little change will occur, frustration will mount, and students will suffer.

COMMON CHALLENGES

In addition to these common and troubling questions often faced, consider just three all-too-common challenges that an effective leader can't afford to ignore.

- It is obvious to you—and reinforced by parent complaints—that very little mathematics learning is taking place in one particular teacher's class. He's a fifth-year teacher who has gotten "acceptable" evaluations, received tenure from your predecessor, and thinks he's doing a good job. What's your plan of attack?

- High-stakes, state-mandated test results for your school are flat over the past three years, far below state averages, and the gaps between racial groups continue to be stark. Your job depends on raising scores and narrowing gaps. Where do you start?

- Your math department believes that scores are low because of the feeder schools' inadequacy and poverty and lack of support from home. They fight you on every proposal you make, knowing that they will outlast you. How do you begin to turn these beliefs around and garner support for change?

Everywhere that improvements have been made and changes implemented, one will find one or more individuals who knew which battles to pick, who mediated conflicts, and who artfully kept the momentum moving and the pressure on. Someone took a potentially dangerous and destructive situation and avoided disaster. Someone listened carefully and responded to the concerns. Someone stepped up and provided leadership.

SUCCESS STORIES

Now consider just a few scenarios of success.

- After a year of piloting new instructional materials, a school system selects a new and somewhat untraditional textbook program. During the first two years of implementation, monthly professional development sessions are held, grade-level meetings are conducted, and teachers are given the opportunity to observe colleagues using these materials. Monthly grade-level meetings are held with the simple agenda of (1) what's working? (2) what's not working? and (3) how best can these issues be addressed? Parents are informed about the program and its strengths and advantages during the pilot year and, once it is adopted, are given frequent updates about the implementation.

■ Challenged to improve adequate, but stagnant, test scores, a school secures a grant to deploy the informally recognized mathematics leader in the school as a full-time school math coach. Systematically balancing co-planning, co-teaching, observing, and performing detailed debriefings with action plans, the coach forges professional bonds with her colleagues and collaboratively focuses on raising the quality of instruction. She steals thirty minutes at each monthly faculty meeting to engage her colleagues in professional learning community activities and, over two years, watches how the improved instruction and more collegial culture translate into higher test scores.

■ Concerned about a history of significant and intractable achievement gaps between primarily white students and primarily minority students, the school board directs administrators to plan and implement a comprehensive initiative to narrow this gap. A blue-ribbon panel comprising teachers, administrators, parents, and community leaders is created. Test scores are disaggregated and carefully analyzed in terms of skills and concepts where gaps do and do not exist. Teachers from high- and low-achieving schools who volunteer are videotaped so that instructional practices can be studied and compared. Finally, a plan involving new forms of professional development, new instructional materials—including state-of-the-art software—and after-school and Saturday support programs is devised and implemented. Two years later, although not eliminated entirely, the gap is half as large and steadily narrowing.

■ Reacting to a lack of improvement in state assessment results, a high school mathematics department recommends the adoption of a new integrated program that has been the source of great controversy in a neighboring community. Letters are sent to parents comparing the new program to the traditional program, honest representations are made about the stagnant test results and unimpressive SAT scores, and a public, teacher-led evening "state of math" session is conducted for parents, the Board of Education, and the community at large.

In every case, a principal or other school leader made the difference. He or she carefully analyzed the situation and strategically planned a course of action. In every case, teachers are active players, partnering with administrators to ensure that the needs and potential concerns of diverse constituencies are addressed early in the change process.

The remainder of this book addresses specific strategies that school leaders like these can use.

▲ informing parents
▲ studying test results for problem areas
▲ closing gaps

2

Making the Case for Change
Strategies and Compelling Examples

One of the responsibilities of leadership, at both the school and district levels, is building a case for change and then presenting this case to teachers, colleagues, parents, and other members of the community in a convincing and compelling manner. Effective leaders convey confidence in the need for changes they advocate. They make their support for these changes clear, and they assure others that careful thought has been given to these decisions.

In the case of reforming and improving school mathematics, principals and other school leaders must use the logic of a geometric proof and the powerful persuasion of effective debate to craft convincing arguments in support of doing things differently. People—particularly the vocal skeptics that we all encounter—need to be reassured that the changes being proposed are based on reason, research, experience, and best thinking, not on the basis of expediency or jumping on the latest bandwagon.

To make a case that is as compelling and convincing as possible, I have often used the following four-part outline:

1. The worlds of work and effective citizenship have changed dramatically, especially as they pertain to the ubiquitous reliance on technology that enhances productivity. It follows that the mathematics that students will need to thrive amid these changes must change as well.

2. The expectations that society sets for schools and the needs that schools are required to meet are higher than ever before. It follows that more students need to master more mathematics just to keep up.

3. Young people are different in important ways from their predecessors of just a few years ago. It follows that the methods used to teach these students must be different from the techniques used for previous generations.

4. There is ample evidence that, despite pockets of excellence and achievement, the traditional program fails to respond to these changing conditions and that mere tinkering at the edges will not produce the mathematical outcomes we need.

In many ways, these are the changes that undergird the impetus and support for the Common Core State Standards. Accordingly, this chapter looks at each of these "domains of rationale" and outlines the process of building the case for the reform of school mathematics programs. Specific strategies for adapting the various components of this outline to one's own situation are presented at the end of each section.

CHANGES IN THE WORLD OF WORK

Because one of the primary purposes of all schooling is to prepare the next generation for productive placement in the workforce, it is reasonable to look at changes in workplace expectations for guidance on why and how to shift school mathematics. Some of the changes are obvious; others are less evident. Among the most obvious changes are those related to an increasingly "high-tech" workplace that requires more mathematical know-how than ever before to maintain productivity and economic competitiveness. It is critical, however, to recognize that what is required is *not* the mathematical know-how of increasingly obsolete skills like factoring trinomials or simplifying radicals. Instead, what are required are increasingly prevalent mathematical understandings like rates of change, statistics, and functions. Less and less are employees called upon to execute calculations with pencil and paper, but more and more are they expected and required to know when and why to perform a particular calculation. Textbooks give students pre-packaged situations and models. The real world expects workers to create and use appropriate models for complex and variable situations!

In fact, the logic for the importance of improving school mathematics programs is reasonably unassailable. The country's long-term economic security and social well-being are clearly linked to sustained innovation and workplace productivity. This innovation and productivity rely, just as clearly, on the quality of human capital and equity of opportunity that, in turn, emerge from high-quality education, particularly in the areas of literacy, mathematics, and science. And high-quality mathematics programs depend on the quality of daily classroom mathematics instruction. Applying the if-then deductive logic of classical geometry puts a strong K–12 mathematics program at the heart of America's long-term economic viability.

Figure 2–1 captures one end of the continuum of what is required in today's world of work. The figure shows an adaptation of a familiar retail establishment's employment test and represents a clear example of entry-level mathematics requirements in today's world. The test prohibits calculators, but look at the balance among the following items:

- two extremely simple computation problems that no one should need a calculator for;
- two word problems that both involve making change; and
- two essay problems that highlight once again of the role of thinking and reasoning.

Employment tests like these are marvelous examples of the fact that some degree of computational skill is still important but that the ability to solve problems and to use thinking and reasoning to explain what you would do and how you would do it are equally important. It is reasonable to ask whether the balance found in this test is reflected by a relatively equivalent balance in one's mathematics curriculum or on the typical tests that students face.

If Figure 2–1 represents entry-level employment, a higher level of expectations, representing the other end of the continuum, can be found in the data generated daily by HMOs and other managed care operations. Surgeons in America today are monitored and evaluated closely on the basis of average cost per patient for such activities as the number of minutes in the operating room, cost of medical and surgical supplies, days in intensive care, and so on. This detailed quantitative analysis of surgeons is but one example of the degree to which nearly all employees face a broad array of data upon which they are expected to make critical decisions. In the case of the HMO data on surgeons, the critical data analysis questions are: What recommendations would you make to each surgeon on the basis of this data? How much confidence would you have in these recommendations? And what additional information would you like to have before making additional suggestions?

I often share examples like this with teachers and parents to help make the case that without significant changes, the traditional skill-based approach to mathematics fails to prepare students for either end of the employment spectrum. I often ask teachers and parents to think about their brothers and sisters, their brothers-in-law and sisters-in-law, and other relatives, and to consider the jobs these family members currently hold. I ask them

Figure 2–1   *Sample employment test for a retail business*

EMPLOYMENT TEST

(No Calculators Please)

1. 20.00
   −5.79

2. 3.59 + 4.88 + .79

3. If a customer's order came to $2.14 and she gave you a $10 bill, what change would you give her?

4. If a customer gave you a $10 bill, a $5 bill, and a quarter for an order that came to $11.21, what change would you give him?

5. What would you do if a customer complained that you gave him too little change?

6. What do you consider to be the two most important qualifications of a retail store employee?

to think about what mathematics is required in these positions and how they think the mathematics is done. I then share the following list of business and industry expectations for school mathematics (National Council of Teachers of Mathematics [NCTM]) 1989, 4) that has been attributed to Henry Pollak, the retired applied mathematician at Bell Labs:

BUSINESS AND INDUSTRY EXPECTATIONS FOR SCHOOL MATHEMATICS:

- the ability to set up problems with the appropriate operations
- knowledge of a variety of techniques to approach and work on problems
- understanding of the underlying mathematical features of a problem
- the ability to work with others on problems
- the ability to see the applicability of mathematical ideas to common and complex problems
- preparation for open problem situations since most real problems are not well formulated
- belief in the utility and value of mathematics

Finally, I ask teachers and parents to reflect on the gap between the traditional expectations of school mathematics programs on the one hand and the newer expectations cited in Pollak's list and in the jobs currently held by their relatives on the other hand.

 STRATEGY 2.1   Use classroom investigations on "How mathematics is used in the world of work" to gather various artifacts like the employment test and HMO data presented here. These materials—rarely limited to just rule-based skills and memorized procedures—serve as excellent ammunition for helping people understand why school mathematics programs must expand their focus on problem solving, communication, and conceptual understanding. A strategically placed "How our parents use mathematics" bulletin board can be a powerful tool for changing perceptions.

THE IMPACT OF TECHNOLOGY

A second category of massive change is the impact of technology—in the form of calculators, computers, and nearly ubiquitous access to the vast resources of the Internet—that has brought databases, spreadsheets, and almost instantaneous access to information of every sort to nearly every home and office, supporting an unprecedented increase in productivity. These changes from a paper-and-pencil world of ledger books to a calculator and computer world of millions, and now even billions, of calculations per second cannot be ignored in the classrooms of America where technology has rendered some mathematics less important while making other mathematics more important than ever, and still other mathematics finally accessible to all.

Just as calculators and computers have changed, if not eliminated, many jobs, they have also changed, if not eliminated, the need for a number of topics in the mathematics curriculum and forced a reconsideration of how this mathematics curriculum is presented. Just as calculators and computers have made employees and businesses far more efficient and productive, these tools can also enhance the efficiency and productivity of teachers and schools. As inconceivable as it is to run a business or industry without cutting-edge technology, it should be equally inconceivable to run schools that are expected to prepare students for the future unless all students and teachers have access to appropriate technology and the skills to make effective use of the tools.

Computers and the Internet are rapidly changing nearly every aspect of our economic and social lives. They are the means by which we communicate, coordinate, and conduct commerce, and they are the engines of massive change. They enhance human capability in nearly every field of endeavor. To believe that students can be denied these tools is to live in a dream world. To believe that technology won't eventually have as great an impact on schools as it does elsewhere in our world is to ignore the sweep of history.

Yet consider how many high-stakes assessments do not allow students to use the very calculators they use to do their homework every evening when they are taking the test. Consider how much time American students spend practicing two- and three-digit-divisor long division of whole numbers and decimals, when an estimate and a calculator-generated answer are such better uses of limited time. Consider how long it takes to grade and return pencil-and-paper assessments that can now be instantaneously graded and reported with available clicker-response technologies. Consider how much effective planning goes into a lesson presented with PowerPoint or on an interactive board and how that lesson is available for reuse and revision for years. And consider how much more efficiently a document camera displays various approaches employed in student work compared to the time that used to be spent copying work onto the blackboard.

When our washing machine breaks down, we turn to an equivalent piece of technology at the Laundromat or we wait for our own to be repaired to get the job done. We no longer resort to the washboard technology that we neither possess nor remember how to use. Similarly, when a calculator is lost or loses battery power, we borrow another calculator, replace the battery, or simply buy a new one. We rarely resort to the paper-and-pencil technology that is either too time consuming or that we no longer remember how to do. It is interesting to note that when the power goes out, for better or worse, the world shuts down. The fact that the power can go out in most of America's schools and education marches on is strong testimony to how little reliance is made on what most consider the greatest enabling variable for change.

STRATEGY 2.2 As part of a data-gathering exercise, ask students to interview their parents and gather information on what tools—one's brain (mental math), pencil and paper, a calculator, or a computer—they use to perform mathematics on the job and at home. Students can generate lists of when their parents are most likely to do mathematics mentally or rely only on estimates, when pencil and paper are still used, and when a calculator or computer is the preferred tool. The graphs and student reports make excellent fodder for presentations and discussions with parents about the reasons for changes in a school's mathematics program.

EFFECTIVE CITIZENSHIP

Third, there are the demands of responsible citizenship—exemplified by understanding such controversial issues as tax policy, solid waste disposal, open space versus the development of suburban sprawl, energy conservation, and crime reduction. To respond intelligently to these and similar issues as well as to assure a truly informed electorate, citizens need an unprecedented degree of mathematical literacy. Jim Rubillo, a former executive director of NCTM, often speaks of "Life's Key Questions." His list includes the following:

- What are the chances?
- What are the risks?
- Are the figures accurate?
- How fast is the situation changing?
- How might things get better or worse?

The answers to each of these questions, and many more, require a deeper and broader understanding of mathematics than ever before.

Accordingly, no matter what one's position is on changing the mathematics curriculum, it is impossible and irresponsible to ignore the facts that tell us daily we are

- bombarded with data that must be organized and analyzed to make informed decisions;
- surrounded by change that must be mathematized to be understood and from which predictions can be made;
- forced to deal with ambiguity and uncertainty that exist in most situations and that can be quantified by using mathematics; and
- confronted in countless situations with a dazzling array of patterns from which we try to make generalizations and draw conclusions.

In case there is any doubt about these realities, just look at some of the following clippings I've collected in the past few years:

- An article in *USA Today* asks: What's in a number? "Does obesity kill 400,000 people a year or 26,000? Do medical mistakes kill 98,000 patients a year or far fewer? The Centers for Disease Control and Prevention (CDC) announced last year that obesity kills 400,000 Americans a year. The CDC last month reduced that estimate to 26,000. The CDC concedes that estimating obesity-related deaths is an 'evolving' science."

- Another article, in which a sports hero takes aim at snuff tobacco, provides statistics on teenagers' use of tobacco (see Figure 2–2).

- The specifications for a generic tablet computer are shown in Figure 2–3.

- A *Washington Post* front-page article announces that 5,000 portable toilets will be available along the National Mall for Barack Obama's inauguration to serve the 1.5 million people expected for the festivities. Don's Johns recommends one toilet for every 100 people. The National Park Service recommends one toilet for every 300, depending upon weather and time of year.

- An article titled: "Cholesterol pill may help the healthy" states:

  After five years, the treated group had 25 percent lower LDL levels and was 37 percent less likely to have suffered a heart attack, unstable angina, or sudden cardiac death. But the actual numbers of such events were quite low in both groups. Five years of lovastatin treatment in 1,000 patients would prevent twelve heart attacks, seven cases of unstable angina, and seventeen bypass or angioplasty procedures, the researchers write.

What more compelling evidence of how important and omnipresent mathematics has become in our society could one ask for? And what more compelling evidence of the gap between real-world mathematics and traditional school mathematics could one find? Look at the mathematical skills and understandings expected of average citizens trying to make informed and wise decisions for themselves and their families.

Figure 2–2 *What do teenagers smoke?*

TEENS' TOBACCO CHOICES

Percent of high school students who said they used tobacco products at least once a month (1997 figures):

	Total	Male	Female
Cigarettes	36.4%	37.7%	34.7%
Smokeless	9.3%	15.8%	1.5%
Cigars	22.0%	31.2%	10.8%

Source: U.S. Centers for Disease Control and Prevention

Figure 2–3   *Specifications for a Generic Tablet Computer*

> ➤ Height: 9 inches (248.5 mm)
> ➤ Width: 7.2 inches (182.9 mm)
> ➤ Depth: 0.4 inch (10.4 mm)
> ➤ Weight: 1.5 pounds (679 g)
> ➤ 9.6-inch (diagonal) LED-backlit glossy widescreen touch display with IPS technology
> ➤ 1024-by-768-pixel resolution at 132 pixels per inch (ppi)
> ➤ 1 GHz dual-core custom-designed, high-performance, low-power system-on-a-chip
> ➤ Back camera: Video recording, HD (720p) up to 30 frames per second with audio; still camera with 5x digital zoom
> ➤ Built-in 25-watt-hour rechargeable lithium-polymer battery
> ➤ Up to 10 hours of surfing the web on Wi-Fi, watching video, or listening to music
> ➤ Up to 10 hours of surfing the web using 3G data network

- Does this array of data make sense? Is any of it intuitively questionable or likely to be wrong?
- How can we get more precise data about the impact of obesity? Which of the two estimates has more validity?
- How can a health campaign use the teenagers tobacco choices data to make a strong case against smoking? What policies should Congress adopt in light of these figures?
- Were there enough portable toilets on the Mall for the inauguration? How big of a problem do you think there was that day?
- How can the tablet computer specifications be used to compare it to other products? Is this particular computer the best buy?
- What additional information would you want before signing up to take lovastatin to lower cholesterol levels?

What clearer evidence could there be that we live in a world of data, a world of change, and a world of ambiguity? And what clearer evidence could there be that the paper-and-pencil, drill-and-practice, memorize-and-regurgitate practices of the traditional mathematics curriculum ill prepare young people to deal with important questions like those asked above?

In short, more than ever, mathematics is everywhere. It is the language of data, the language of change, and the language of patterns. It is the tool that is used to quantify situations and the language that helps us make sense of phenomena. It is the gut conceptual understanding of the magnitude of numbers, of a sense of what is likely or unlikely, of what is reasonable or unreasonable, and of what's changing and how fast. It is *not* a set of memorized procedures that are now almost universally done by machine, nor an array of Trivial-Pursuit-like formulas that are rarely retained ten minutes after the exam. It is this increasingly ubiquitous nature of mathematics, in conjunction with its longstanding practicality, that makes changing what we teach, how we teach it, and how we assess it so imperative.

Hopefully, these examples and suggested strategies help people reach the conclusion that today's requirements of productive work, the impact of technology, and the demands of effective citizenship provide a strong basis for commensurate changes in what mathematics must be valued and taught to students who will live most of their lives in the twenty-first century. Moreover, these varied examples provide support for adoption of the Common Core State Standards for Mathematics and the long-overdue emphasis on making sense of numbers, applying mathematics, modeling and reasoning with mathematics, and analyzing data that one finds highlighted in the new standards.

STRATEGY 2.3 As seen in the *USA Today* and *Washington Post* examples, newspapers and assorted news websites are often a cornucopia of data that beg interpretation and examples of how mathematics is required in the real world. An interesting experiment to conduct (or to challenge others to conduct) is to compare the percentage of time or pages allocated to specific mathematics topics found in the traditional curriculum with the percentage of times these same mathematics topics are found in the news, business, sports, and entertainment pages of the local newspaper. People are often astounded at how poor a match one finds.

CHANGES IN EXPECTATIONS

Perhaps even more important than better meeting the needs of a changing workplace and society is the increasing necessity for mathematics to meet the needs of a much greater percentage of students than has ever before been the case.

It used to be so easy. Teachers lectured and students listened. Teachers showed students how to get answers, and students then practiced the procedures. Homework and tests were based largely on memorization of these procedures and application came last, if at all. Some learned; many failed. Some enjoyed this ritual; many still suffer from its scars. But most important, the system ensured that the smart got smarter, the average stayed average, and the weakest never caught on or up. For most of the 1950s, '60s, and even '70s, this arrangement worked. Schools did a magnificent job of meeting society's needs for a few mathematically gifted citizens, a few more mathematically able, and most with only limited mathematical understanding. Just look at how the mathematics curriculum has been used to sort students into "winners" and "losers."

■ Second graders have been expected to master subtraction with regrouping using only symbols, despite their limited understanding of either place value or addition and subtraction facts, leading many to a premature self-concept of being mathematically inept. The Common Core State Standards for Mathematics moves the standard algorithm for subtraction to third grade!

■ Paper-and-pencil proficiency with fractions continues to be a prerequisite for the study of algebra, despite the fact that most key algebraic ideas require little or no skill with fractions. The Common Core State Standards for Mathematics systematically presents a learning progression from grade 3 to grade 5 that effectively blends conceptual understanding of fractions supported by an array of appropriate representations with the skills of fraction computation that become "rules with understanding" in place of rules to be memorized without understanding or adequate prerequisite knowledge.

■ The critical study of functions, statistics, and trigonometry are too often denied to students unable to master the arithmetic of polynomials or the simplification of rational expressions, despite the fact that the former requires very little of the latter. The Common Core State Standards for Mathematics includes high and appropriate expectations at both the middle school and high school levels for the development of understanding of functions and statistics by all students.

■ Conversely, a range of topics like complex numbers, vectors, and trigonometric identities have limited value for most students who have few plans or little likelihood of majoring in science, engineering, or mathematics. That is why the Common Core State Standards for Mathematics, at the high school level, propose 113 grades 9–12 standards for *all* students and an additional 43 "+" standards for STEM-intending students that are not deemed essential for all students.

In each of these cases, the mathematics curriculum has presented road blocks that have effectively kept many from moving on. We have implemented a curriculum that has systematically set up both teachers and students, guaranteeing that only a few will succeed. And it bears repeating: For many years, this arrangement worked for schools, worked for society, and resulted in nearly none of the concerns or criticisms so widespread today. The good news is that the Common Core State Standards for Mathematics is removing many of these road blocks and finally providing more opportunity for all.

Another way that the interaction between students and school mathematics plays out is captured in a most compelling fashion in *Everybody Counts:*

> Virtually all young children like mathematics. They do mathematics natural-ly, discovering patterns and making conjectures based on observation. Natural curiosity is a powerful teacher, especially for mathematics. Unfortunately, as children become socialized by school and society, they begin to view math-ematics as a rigid system of externally dictated rules governed by standards of accuracy, speed, and memory. Their view of mathematics shifts gradually from enthusiasm to apprehension, from confidence to fear. Eventually, most students leave mathematics under duress, convinced that only geniuses can learn it. Later, as parents, they pass this conviction on to their children. Some

even become teachers and convey this attitude to their students. (National Research Council [NRC]) 1989, 43–44)

But just as the need for universal reading literacy forced schools to adopt new curricula and new instructional techniques to expand the proportion of students leaving schools as successful readers, so too must schools now adopt similar changes in mathematics curricula to reach new levels of mathematical literacy.

STRATEGY 2.4 Conduct a discussion at a faculty meeting or a mathematics department meeting on ways in which students are sorted in our school and ways in which the opportunities students have are limited by our policies and practices—often created with the best of intentions. List these policies and practices, identify the obstacles (both overt and covert) that have been erected, and discuss the implications of changing these practices or removing some of these obstacles. (For example, the practice of using reading scores as a criterion for entry into eighth-grade algebra has a long history and interesting implications. Similarly, the practice of pulling weaker students out of mainstream mathematics instruction for supplemental—and other less rigorous—instruction clearly communicates different expectations.)

CHANGES IN STUDENTS

An often forgotten—or conveniently ignored—piece of the puzzle is the students themselves and the enormous changes in the experiences and attitudes with which they arrive in school. We all recognize that today's student

- has lived in a wireless, interconnected world for all or most of his or her life;
- seamlessly juggles text messages, e-mail, downloaded music and video, and everything else the Internet has to offer on a piece of technology that slides into a pocket;
- has essentially instantaneous access, via Google, to nearly all the facts, answers, and explanations that school demands; and
- has grown up with an assortment of fast-paced video games, the pulsating rap of hip-hop, and the zaniness of reality TV shows.

It is well known to any classroom teacher that the days of a well-mannered class sitting quietly and obediently in rows, completing page after page of calculations are long gone. But rather than dream wistfully for those "good old days," it is necessary to compare the fast-paced, highly visual world of today's students with the equally fast-paced, computer-driven world of commerce with its e-mails, smart phones, faxes, pagers, and FedExes.

To bolster this argument, consider some facets of today's reality.

- American youth spend much more time per year in front of electronic screens in their homes—TV, computers, and video games—than they spend in school.

- In homes with children, Internet access is more commonplace than newspapers and magazines.

- Many teenagers would give up TV before giving up their computer or the Internet.

- Cable TV took twenty-five years to get to 10 million subscribers. The VCR took nine years. The World Wide Web only five years! iPods, iPhones, and iPads and their cousins, even faster!

In the face of cultural changes of this magnitude, it is impossible to believe that school mathematics can be immune to change as well. But sometimes the case is best made closer to home where it was not uncommon to find my rather typical teenager at his computer juggling several Internet sites from which he was downloading material for a social studies paper he was writing, two instant messages from friends, and a slew of e-mail messages to which he was in the process of responding. I am often struck by how similar this fast-paced electronic world is to the prevailing environment of offices and businesses I frequent, and how different it is from most schools and classrooms. Is it any wonder that he and so many others are so bored in school? Isn't it amazing that one of the most common concerns at focus groups on textbook design is how "busy" the pages look? Isn't it time to recognize and address the growing gap between our students' real lives and their lives in school? Isn't it time to narrow the gap between the realities of the world of work and the realities of the typical mathematics program? Isn't it time to provide electronic textbooks?

Thus, not only do the critics of reform conveniently ignore how much the world has changed, more dangerous, they fail to acknowledge how much our children have changed. In clinging to the traditions of the past and ignoring the impact of the Internet, fast-paced video games, and a culture driven by the incessant beat of MTV, rap, and hip-hop, the skeptics condemn the next generation to mathematics instruction too often unrelenting its boredom, astounding in its irrelevance, and frightening in its ability to demean and demoralize!

STRATEGY 2.5 Since many people, including parents and teachers, are often surprisingly oblivious to the magnitude of change in students themselves, it is often useful to gather data as part of mathematics instruction that can also be used to better inform adults about today's students. Teachers can be encouraged to share survey data that students collect and summarize on such topics as

- ➤ the interests of students in our class versus contexts found in the problems in our math book;
- ➤ the number of calculators and computers found in my home and how they are used;
- ➤ five things I enjoy doing and why; and five things I don't enjoy doing and why.

Such data makes for powerful fodder in principal newsletters, on school bulletin boards, and at parent meetings. As in the world of business, such data is comparable to "knowing one's customers." It can be used to better meet the needs of these "customers" as well as provide a rationale for those changes that are required to better meet these needs.

Once again, the evidence is clear. As expectations have been raised and as students have changed in significant ways, one must face the obvious conclusion that the mathematics we teach and the manner in which we teach it must undergo commensurate changes to respond appropriately. Chapter 3 begins to describe these changes in detail.

WHAT THE TRADITIONAL PROGRAM HATH WROUGHT

This next task of debunking the so-called accomplishments of the traditional program is perhaps the most difficult—but perhaps the most important—part of making a case for change. After all, there are pockets of success, even excellence, within all school and districts. In addition, we have all spent so much time putting the best spin on even mediocre results that suggesting that all is not well can be a daunting task. However, many parents and skeptics assume that an easy solution is merely to continue to do all that we have been doing and just to add on a little more that is new. Such a compromised approach ignores the fact that some of what we have been doing is no longer needed and some has never really worked well at all.

One way to make the point that there really were "no good old days" and that the traditional program has a long history of failure is to collect anecdotal tidbits that reveal the seriousness of the mathematics achievement problem. Several of my favorite examples follow.

Once again, our daily newspapers often provide the best insight into just how serious the problem is, as is seen in the snippet from the *San Jose Mercury News*:

> And some food companies have started rewriting recipes after calls from
> customers who fail to grasp that a 9×13 baking pan is the same as a 13×9 pan.
> And that egg whites are not egg shells.

It's fairly obvious what happens when measurement topics are subordinated to mindless computational procedures, or worse, when the measurement chapter is skipped entirely. So we must recognize the consequences of making the mistake of maintaining a curriculum that has never produced widespread mathematical literacy.

In addition to the myth of some glorious return to some nonexistent past, there is the daily confrontation with how society's need for mathematical know-how is seriously outpacing the extant quantity of such know-how. One does not have to look far for examples of how number sense, measurement, and statistical deficiencies come home to roost. Consider the shamefully common events described on the front page of the January 25, 1995, *Waterbury (CT) American*, which featured a photograph of a large tractor trailer stuck under an overpass. Under the headline "Faulty Bridge Sign Traps Truck" one reads:

> When city workers measured a bridge over West Main Street last fall, their
> efforts fell a little short—10 inches short to be exact. After yet another tractor
> trailer got wedged beneath the railroad bridge near Sperry Street, Traffic De-
> partment workers decided to remeasure the clearance Wednesday morning.
> To their surprise, the clearance is 10 inches shorter than the 13 feet, 8 inches
> noted on the warning sign before the bridge.

The clearance is 12 feet 10 inches. Sgt. John Hyland, the city's traffic engineer, said employees of the paint and sign division measured the bridge in September or October, and that the new signs were installed January 18 to replace the old ones. He said the person or people who made the mistake will face disciplinary action.

Saturday night, an 18-wheeler driven by John E. Thomas, 35, of Waterbury got stuck beneath the bridge. He was able to drive the truck, measuring 13 feet, 6 inches in height, back to the Sorensen Transportation Co. in Bethany. Thomas, who was hired by the company in November, said he was terminated from his job Monday because the accident happened during his 3-month probation.

All because of one little measurement error!

For anyone not yet convinced that there is a mathematics achievement problem that rears its ugly head in more and more inconvenient and even dangerous ways, consider

- how frustrating it is when your car is "repaired" by a high school dropout who used to tune an engine with merely an ear and a wrench and who now must rely on a digital readout to accurately tune today's high-tolerance and highly finicky engines; or

- how scary it is that the overnight maintenance on the commercial jet's engines might have been completed by someone with less than a full understanding of the difference between 0.1 and 0.01; or

- how deadly it can be when hospital ICUs are staffed with people whose understanding of the metric system and of proportions can lead to serious errors in calculating drug doses and IV drip rates.

And then, there's the following letter I received in the mail.

Dear Steve,

I am an attorney. About ten years ago, I was working for a small firm in New Britain when my boss assigned me a case involving the defense of a drunk driver. The defendant had been arrested after a routine traffic stop (there had been no accident). After checking the vehicle's registration, the defendant was given the field sobriety tests. After failing the walk-a-straight-line and touch-your-nose tests, he was given a breath test, which registered 0.13 (0.10 being the legal limit). At the police station, he consented to a blood test, which registered 0.15.

Here are the facts:

1. Connecticut's drunken driving law requires that the operator exceed the legal limit while operating his or her motor vehicle.

2. Twenty minutes after last operating a motor vehicle, the defendant had a blood alcohol level of .13, and sixty minutes after last operating a motor vehicle, his level was .15.

3.   Therefore, his level was increasing and there is no way to be sure that he was above .10 when he was operating the motor vehicle.

His case was dismissed!

Obviously, there is a basic flaw in my argument: Both .13 and .15 are squarely within the standard deviations of both tests. In fact, from a purely statistical analysis, the tests were consistent and proved beyond a reasonable doubt that my client was drunk. Interestingly enough, the prosecutor missed the flaw, but the judge did not. Why the dismissal, then? The judge told me: "I know that your argument is faulty, but I also know that the prosecution will never in a million years be able to convince a jury of that fact. No jury will understand the numbers, and therefore, no jury would convict your client."

The bottom line here is that a drunk driver slipped through the cracks and is free to drive a car because of rampant mathematical illiteracy!

Just think how easy it should be for the prosecutors of the world to turn to a flipchart before the jury and pencil in the data:

20 minutes — .13 blood alcohol content

60 minutes — .15 blood alcohol content

And then, with a knowing and dignified flourish, the prosecutor sketches a vertical and horizontal axis. What a wonderful picture can be conjured up of "mathematics-to-the-rescue" as the prosecutor plots (20, .13) and (60, .15) and connects them with a line that clearly passes above .10 on the vertical Blood Alcohol Content axis!

But alas, when jury members have been deprived of the opportunity to study algebra or when jury members' primary algebraic experiences entailed the mindless simplification of radicals and rational expressions instead of a healthy dose of data analysis, there is little hope for conviction of the guilty and protection of the innocent.

Figure 2–4   *The prosecutor rebuttal: Time versus blood alcohol content*

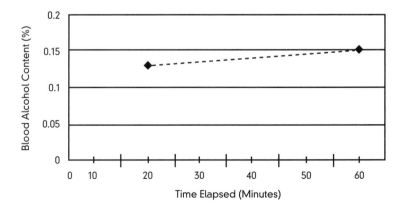

STRATEGY 2.6   In addition to using examples like the previous ones verbatim or similar examples drawn from local media, principals and other school leaders can often find powerful ammunition in school and district test results on released items. It is not uncommon to find reasonably high scores on relatively low-level types of items entailing merely recall of vocabulary and memorized procedures. However, sharing relatively higher-level items—with usually much lower scores—can help rally both understanding and support for a stronger and more relevant curriculum.

SUMMING UP

By now the logic should be irrefutable: The world has changed dramatically. Since schools are expected to prepare young people for the world they will face, what we do in schools to prepare students for this changing world must change as well. Unfortunately, this needed role of preparing students for the future directly conflicts with the traditional role of schools serving to perpetuate the rich mores, lore, and traditions of our culture. And here is where the trouble begins. We find people equating the place of, say, the Revolutionary War in the curriculum with, say, the place of long division. Both represent important traditions of our culture. However, one (obviously, the Revolutionary War) is as interesting and as important today as it was yesterday, while the other (obviously, long division) is increasingly obsolete and serves no useful purpose in meeting the future needs students will face. To build an effective case for change, principals and other school leaders must use the magnitude of change in society at large as ammunition when addressing the implications of these changes on mathematics programs and support commensurate changes in the mathematics programs.

3

Responding to These Changes
What to Expect and Advocate

Ideally, the ideas and strategies described in the previous chapter set the stage for change. Hopefully, they create a foundation for which there is general agreement that

- the magnitude of the changes in the world of work are large;
- mathematical literacy is a more important intellectual commodity than ever before;
- this literacy must be developed in a much higher proportion of students than ever before;
- expectations must rise to keep pace with these changes;
- students themselves and their motivations have changed significantly as well; and
- traditional approaches are unlikely to satisfy these changing conditions.

Now it's time for the heavy lifting. Given all of these changes, it should follow naturally that the mathematics curriculum must shift, instructional practices must be adjusted, methods of assessing understanding must be altered, and professional growth and support for teachers must be strengthened. It's one thing to call for shifts and changes. It's quite another to implement them. Before embarking on this process of implementation and change, principals and other school leaders must understand clearly what each of these shifts entails and what each would look like in classrooms. Only then can one articulately and effectively advocate for such changes. What follows are encapsulated descriptions and examples of each of these shifts.

CURRICULUM SHIFTS

In an abbreviated form, the heart of the revision to the K–12 mathematics curriculum stems from a clarion call for a "shift in emphasis from a curriculum dominated by an emphasis on memorization of isolated facts and procedures, and proficiency with paper and pencil skills, to one which emphasizes conceptual understandings, multiple representations and connections, mathematical modeling and mathematical problem solving" (NCTM 1989, 125). NCTM first laid out this vision in broad grade-band strokes over twenty years ago and left it to districts and states to fill in the details. Now the Common Core State Standards for Mathematics codifies this shift with a coherent set of grade-level expectations that balance skills and concepts—what student need to do and what students need to know—and a set of standards for mathematical practice that capture how students should learn mathematics.

More specifically, at the K–8 level, this means a mathematics curriculum that emphasizes the applications of adding, subtracting, multiplying, and dividing whole numbers, decimals, and fractions in the contexts of buying and selling, comparing, measuring, predicting, and interpreting, thereby giving students reasons to care about learning. Similarly, at the 9–12 level, this means a curriculum that replaces the primary emphasis on rules and procedures for manipulating symbols—tasks that are nearly always done today with technological tools—with an emphasis on using and applying mathematical concepts to formulate and solve a broad range of problems that arise in diverse situations entailing quantity, data, change, patterns, optimizing, scaling, measuring, predicting, and proving.

Figure 3–1 suggests a rationale for this curricular shift from a focus on procedures to a focus on creating and using mathematical models—that is, for example, from a focus on merely *how* to divide whole numbers to a focus on *when* and *why* to use the operation of division. It attempts to convey the changing focus from procedures that are memorized to models that are understood, created, and applied. This figure also attempts to clarify the ongoing interplay among grounding mathematics in the real world (situations and phenomena), mathematical symbols and language (mathematical representations), and finally solutions. In a world without calculators and computers it makes sense for mathematics to focus primarily on the right-hand side of the diagram, that is, the use of well-practiced and memorized procedures to convert mathematical representations to answers. However, in a world where calculators and computers do most procedural mathematics, we must shift our curricular focus to the left-hand side of the diagram, that is, the use of mathematical models to convert diverse situations and phenomena into appropriate mathematical representations. That is why mathematical modeling plays such a prominent role in the Common Core State Standards and why this shift will be such a challenge to accomplish.

In the classroom, some of the implications of this shift are captured in Figures 3–2 and 3–3. One shows the shift from long division to using division to solve interesting problems. The other shows the shift from an algebra course driven by manipulating symbols to one driven by solving problems that develop algebraic thinking. Note how little the "where we've beens" relate to the Common Core standards for mathematical practice. Then note how the "where we're moving tos" represent the magnitude of the shift that is implied by a focus on problem solving, reasoning, justification, and modeling.

gure 3–1   *Shifting the curriculum*

SITUATIONS AND PHENOMENA	MATHEMATICAL MODELS	MATHEMATICAL REPRESENTATIONS	MATHEMATICAL PROCEDURES	SOLUTIONS
(such as the lottery, gravity, interest, queuing, or trajectories) are converted using appropriate	(such as multiplication, exponentiation, proportion, or linear function) into	(such as a diagram, a table, a graph, an expression, or an equation) which in turn are converted using appropriate	(such as long division, squaring, factoring, solving, or proving) into	(such as answers, explanations, justifications, or proofs)

gure 3–2   *Long division: Then and now*

WHERE WE'VE BEEN:	WHERE WE'RE MOVING TO:
Using pencil and paper, find the quotient: $$1.59 \div 10$$	Given the data: *Cheeseburgers cost $1.59 each and you have $10.00* With calculators available, consider and answer the following questions. In each case, show your work and explain how you arrived at your answer. ➤ Can you afford to buy 10? Why or why not? ➤ How many can you afford to buy? Did you remember to include tax? ➤ At what sales tax rate can you afford an additional cheeseburger? ➤ Explain how you arrived at your answer. ➤ Create two additional questions that arise from this situation and this data.

gure 3–3   *Algebra: Then and now*

WHERE WE'VE BEEN:	WHERE WE'RE MOVING TO:

For the past forty years, algebra has been a course that students and teachers have raced through, built around a series of units or chapters on the topics:
 	
    signed numbers
 	
    variables and expressions
 	
    equations
 	
    linear functions
	Algebraic skills and concepts embedded into grades 7, 8, and 9 where students and teachers have time to focus on big ideas and applications built around a series of units or chapters on the following topics:
	
	    the language of algebra: variables, expressions, and integers
	
	    patterns, equations, and functions
	
	    variable situations leading to linear equations and functions
	
	    creating and applying linear functions

(continues)

Figure 3–3   *Algebra: Then and now (continued)*

WHERE WE'VE BEEN:	WHERE WE'RE MOVING TO:
polynomials and exponents factoring rational expressions systems of equations quadratic equations Algebra of this sort has been assessed with test items that primarily asked students to simplify solve factor graph	data, trend lines, and the graphing tools proportions and variation—lines in the form of y = bx and curves in the form of xy = b systems of equations and matrices exponential functions—multiplicative change versus additive change linear programming Algebra of this sort will be assessed with test items that primarily asked students to express display solve represent explain organize demonstrate model

In both cases, the essence of this curricular shift is captured in one of the overarching objectives of mathematics—then and now—presented in Figure 3–4.

Figure 3–4   *Overarching mathematics objective: Then and now*

OVERARCHING K–8 MATHEMATICS CURRICULUM OBJECTIVE **THEN:**	OVERARCHING K–8 MATHEMATICS CURRICULUM OBJECTIVE **NOW:**
Given a numerical computation problem, students will use pencil and paper and the appropriate algorithm to find the sum, difference, product, or quotient.	Given a problem situation with realistic data, the student will decide which operation (addition, subtraction, multiplication, or division) is appropriate to use and then explain why that key on the calculator will help determine a useful quantitative result for the given problem and why that answer is reasonable.

One of the examples I use to help crystallize the need for this shift is the following excerpt from an article on dealing with jet lag that I stumbled upon several years ago in the *USAir Magazine*:

Synchronizing the internal clock to local time generally takes from one to one and a half days per time zone (though for some people it can take twice as long). For example, Tokyo is 14 time zones removed from New York, so it will take the average person nine days to adjust ($14 \div 1.5 = 9$).

Imagine my surprise when I wrestled with the discrepancy between my estimate of fourteen to twenty-one days (one to one and a half days for each of fourteen times zones) and the nine days asserted it the article. And how dare a reader question the supporting equation that apparently justifies the answer of nine days! But what better evidence can one find to help make the case that we have a serious mathematics achievement problem? The excerpt reminds us vividly that we have taught the average and below average students *how* to divide (14 divided by 1.5 is indeed 9), but we have not taught enough students the far more important skills of deciding *when* and *why* to divide. Taken even further, the excerpt reminds us that we have taught most student how to get *answers to exercises* in preparation for a world that increasing requires people to arrive at *solutions to problems*.

Laying the Readiness Foundation Strategy

Clearly, change of this magnitude, implicit in the curriculum shifts required by the Common Core State Standards for Mathematics (CCSSM), requires familiarity with exactly what is changing and how it is changing. Teachers at all levels need time and support to analyze these changes. One approach to this is to engage teachers at each grade level and for each course in discussions about

- exactly which and what proportion of the CCSSM are fully and/or partially matched by existing standards at that grade—that is, what is essentially the same or superficially the same, but deeper;
- exactly which and what proportion of the CCSSM are fully and/or partially matched by existing standards at a different grade—that is, what has to be moved;
- exactly which and what proportion of the CCSSM are not matched by existing standards at any grade—that is, what is new content; and
- exactly which current state standards for any grade or course get moved to a different grade or are no longer expected to be taught.

As we'll discuss in later chapters, a key role of school leaders is supporting these discussions so that rather than another imposition of curricular change from above, there are substantive collegial discussions about the specific grade level and course implications of the Common Core State Standards for Mathematics.

The Baby and the Bath Water Strategy

Another effective approach that teachers and administrators can use to help make curriculum decisions is to systematically examine what mathematics is still important to know and what is no longer important. We are often reminded not to "throw the baby out with the bath water." Less frequently are we reminded that what was once recognized as "baby" may now increasingly be "bath water." Therefore, one way to grasp the changes described in this chapter is to see reform as an ongoing analysis of what components of the mathematics curriculum are still fully part of the "baby" and which components of the curriculum are either clearly or increasingly part of the "bath water" that is best thrown away.

Here's a way to start these discussions. Despite what some have claimed, a mastery of one-digit number facts has always been a critical part of the "baby" and continues to be a critical part of the "baby." No set of standards and no framework from California to Connecticut has suggested abandoning mastery of number facts. Given that these facts (e.g., $17 - 8 = 9$, $7 \times 4 = 28$) are indispensable for estimation and for mental computation, and given that these facts are essential for building number sense, it is inconceivable—even in a world of calculators—that they would be cast aside with the "bath water." In fact, mastery of number facts is more important than ever. But, if, for the first time in our history, *all* students are going to master these facts, we must expand our teaching repertoire beyond memorization and practice. Facts must be approached in contexts (e.g., simple price lists), with materials (e.g., counters, number lines, even fingers), via fact families (e.g., $4 \times 7 + 28$, $7 \times 4 = 28$, $28 \div 4 = 7$ and $28 \div 7 = 4$, to reduce memory load), and with attention to strategies ($8 + 9 = 17$ because $8 + 9$ is the same as $8 + 8$ or 16 plus 1 or the same as $8 + 10$ or 18 minus 1).

In the case of multidigit paper-and-pencil computation the situation is reversed. Given all of the changes we face and the need to expand the scope of the curriculum, it is time that multiplication and division with factors and divisors containing three or more digits and computation with fractions and mixed numbers with denominators like 7, 9, 11, or 13 finally be relegated as "bath water." Just as we have survived dropping the square root algorithm from the curriculum—but increased the emphasis on the concept of square root—we can and will survive the elimination of increasingly obsolete, multidigit computation. Students able to use one of several appropriate algorithms to multiply and divide by one- and two-digit factors and divisors will ably meet the expectations of the Common Core State Standards for Mathematics.

One effective method for helping to make these "baby versus bath water" decisions is to ask the question: Is this something what I want my own child to be able to do? When I realized that I was far more upset that my twelve-year-old couldn't estimate the difference between $7\frac{1}{5}$ and $4\frac{6}{7}$ (with a practical answer of a little more than 2) than whether he could correctly calculate the difference (a precise, but absurd $2\frac{12}{35}$), I began to clarify where the "baby–bath water" line was.

So at its core, which curricular shifts we choose to make reflect what we value. It is increasingly clear to me what I value and what the CCSSM values. It is the role of principals and other school leaders to clarify and publicize what they believe, to engage teachers in discussions about their core values, and to use these beliefs and values to make and defend their decisions about mathematics curriculum, instruction, and assessment.

The following are some skills that are valued now and will clearly be valued in the future:

- Calculate with appropriate accuracy
- Express ideas using mathematically appropriate language
- Solve word problems
- Make reasonable estimates
- Explain one's reasoning
- Measure, construct, devise, and display
- Defend decisions and positions
- Solve nonroutine problems
- Formulate and solve your own problems

INSTRUCTIONAL SHIFTS

The curriculum shifts discussed earlier must be supported by changes in instructional practices as well. Once again, *Everybody Counts* says it most compellingly:

> Evidence from many sources shows that the least effective mode for mathematics learning is the one that prevails in most of America's classrooms: lecturing and listening. Despite daily homework, for most students and most teachers, mathematics continues to be primarily a passive activity: teachers prescribe, students transcribe. Students simply do not retain for long what they learn by imitation from lectures, worksheets, or routine homework. Presentation and repetition help students do well on standardized tests and lower-order skills, but they are generally ineffective as teaching strategies for long-term learning, for higher-order thinking, and for versatile problem solving." (NRC 1989, 57)

Instead, our vision for mathematics instruction, supported by both research and the wisdom of practice, involves classrooms where students are regularly asking appropriate questions, engaging in sustained work, and investigating to make personal sense of mathematical ideas.

For example, instead of merely posing the problem: $92 - 37 = ?$ and expecting that students will proceed in step-by-step fashion to regroup the 92 into 8 tens and 12 ones in order to "correctly" find the difference, the instructional shift that is essential would include much of what is shown in Figure 3–5. Notice that this instruction includes, but goes well beyond, getting a correct answer. It also involves problem solving, understanding the meaning of subtraction, estimation, and, most important, alternative approaches to arrive at estimates and answers—in other words, instruction that blends the content standards and the standards for mathematical practice found in the Common Core State Standards for Mathematics.

Figure 3–5   *Shifting instruction*

Given: 92 − 37 = ?

Teachers might ask:

1. Write a real-world problem, using realistic data, that would require someone to find this difference.

2. For the different problems that students create:

➤ What is a reasonable estimate for your problem?

➤ How did you get your estimate?

➤ What is the actual answer to your problem?

➤ Explain how you arrived at your answer.

The Third International Mathematics and Science Study (TIMSS) videotaped eighth-grade classes in the United States, Germany, and Japan. The videos reinforced the need for these instructional shifts in the United States. They powerfully model the steps in typical eighth-grade mathematics lessons in these countries. Figure 3–6 summarizes the differences in the common lesson scripts found in these countries and strongly supports movement toward what is typically found in Japanese classrooms, which consistently produce higher levels of student achievement than American classrooms.

Figure 3–6   *Comparison of the steps typical of eighth-grade mathematics lessons in Japan, the United States, and Germany*

THE EMPHASIS ON UNDERSTANDING IS EVIDENT IN THE STEPS TYPICAL OF JAPANESE EIGHTH-GRADE MATHEMATICS LESSONS:

Teacher poses a complex, thought-provoking problem.

Students struggle with the problem.

Various students present ideas or solutions to the class.

Class discusses the various solution methods.

The teacher summarizes the class' conclusions.

Students practice similar problems.

IN CONTRAST, THE EMPHASIS ON SKILL ACQUISITION IS EVIDENT IN THE STEPS COMMON TO MOST U.S. AND GERMAN MATH LESSONS:

Teacher instructs students in a concept or skill.

Teacher solves example problems with class.

Students practice on their own while the teacher assists individual students.

Source: Third International Mathematics and Science Study

Another way of capturing the essence of the shifts that are needed in our mathematics instruction can be extracted from the far less controversial world of the reading curriculum. It is widely accepted that effective reading instruction and assessment builds from literal comprehension to inferential comprehension to evaluative comprehension. There is widespread understanding that to be deemed powerful readers, all students must be exposed to and must master all three types of comprehension. In contrast, much of mathematics instruction begins and ends with literal comprehension, that is, the mathematical equivalent of "Who went to the store with Bobby?" Effective mathematics instruction must be expanded to include inferential comprehension and evaluative comprehension like that embodied in the questions in Figure 3–7.

Figure 3–7   *Reading and mathematics comprehension parallels*

Literal comprehension:	What is the answer? What are you being asked to find?
Inferential comprehension:	Why do you suppose Keisha multiplied? What conclusion can you draw from that data?
Evaluative comprehension:	Is Sam's answer reasonable? Why or why not? Why would you want to know that?

The progression of questioning in good instruction can be captured very simply. When pencils cost 3¢ each and pens cost 4¢ each, the following set of questions and answers demonstrate an instructional shift that goes beyond just requiring a correct answer. Note how instead of stopping at the correct answer, the teacher pushes instruction to higher-order questions that focus on the student's broader understanding and ability to explain.

Teacher:	How much will it cost to purchase one pencil and one pen?
Student:	7¢.
Teacher:	Good, how did you get 7¢?
Student:	I added.
Teacher:	Great. Why did you add?
Student:	Because I needed both items and you add when you put things together.

Or at a higher level:

> **Teacher:**   What would the graph of that situation look like?
> **Student:**   It would start at the origin and move up and to the right.
> **Teacher:**   Good, what can you say about the slope of your graph?
> **Student:**   It's positive.
> **Teacher:**   Great. Why do you think it's positive?
> **Student:**   Because when one variable gets bigger, so does the other.

The instructional shifts described in these two simple vignettes can be categorized as methods of fostering a thinking and reasoning curriculum, that is, a curriculum that values correct answers, not as an end unto themselves but as a means to do and learn so much more.

NCTM's *Professional Standards for Teaching Mathematics* reiterates these points when it advocates mathematics teaching that empowers all students by shifting toward the following:

- Classrooms as mathematical communities—away from classrooms as simply a collection of individuals
- Logic and mathematical evidence as verification—away from the teacher as the sole authority for right answers
- Mathematical reasoning—away from merely memorizing procedures
- Conjecturing, inventing, and problem solving—away from an emphasis on mechanistic answer-finding
- Connecting mathematics, its ideas, and its applications—away from treating mathematics as a body of isolated concepts and procedures

The "Let's Go to the Video" Strategy

An all too infrequently used approach that teachers and administrators can use to help examine and shift instructional practices is to videotape and collegially discuss selected lessons. Sometimes it is safest and easiest to go online and turn to videos available on websites like Inside Mathematics (www.insidemathematics.org) or the Annenburg Mathematics Video Library (www.learner.org), which include sets of videos that model standards-based instruction at the elementary, middle, and high school levels. Once teachers see the value of using videos and once they are comfortable sharing their successes and failures, actual videos of classroom instruction from one's own school are often the most powerful way to stimulate discussion about what is being done, what isn't being done, and what could be done to improve instruction. We must recognize that while curriculum and assessment can be written down and read, instruction can be observed only as it is occurring or captured for later viewing on video. Figure 3–8 shows the six-item protocol that I have used with teachers to engage in safe analysis of their teaching.

Figure 3–8   *What to look for when analyzing a video of a mathematics lesson*

➤ The richness and appropriateness of the **tasks, problems, and examples**
  ◆ Tasks are aligned with the overall learning goal or objective.
  ◆ Mathematically meaningful tasks are selected.
  ◆ Relevant contexts are used.
  ◆ Tasks are appropriately sequenced.

➤ The quality and clarity of the **explanations**
  ◆ Accurate definitions are used.
  ◆ The focus is on why procedures and processes work.
  ◆ Explanations are clear and make sense.
  ◆ Alternative approaches are used and valued.
  ◆ Attention is given to misconceptions and mistakes.

➤ The effectiveness and appropriateness of **representations**
  ◆ Representations used are appropriate.
  ◆ Multiple representations are used.
  ◆ Different representations are connected.

➤ The frequency with which students are asked **"Why?"**
  ◆ "Why?" "Can you explain that?" "How do you know?" are commonplace.
  ◆ Questions consistently probe for student understanding and thinking.

➤ The gathering of **evidence of learning**, i.e., formative assessment
  ◆ Lessons conclude with summary and/or debriefing.
  ◆ Lessons conclude with an appropriate "exit slip" that reveals the degree to which the learning goal has been met.

➤ The maintenance of a focus on the **big mathematical ideas and concepts**
  ◆ Connections are made to how concepts are related.
  ◆ Explanations for procedures are grounded in concepts.

ASSESSMENT SHIFTS

The glue that holds the entire system of curriculum and instruction together is the content and format of the assessment used to evaluate whether and how well things are working. If curriculum and instruction are to change in ways that have been described earlier, then assessment must change as well. When the emphasis of the mathematics curriculum moves toward concepts and problem solving, a parallel move must occur in the assessments used to measure student achievement. Similarly, when the emphasis of mathematics instruction shifts toward connections and communication, in addition to correct answers, a parallel shift must occur in the assessments that teachers and school use. That is why NCTM has advocated "a shift in the vision of evaluation toward a system based on evidence from multiple sources and away from relying on evidence from a single test as well as a shift toward relying on the professional judgments of teachers and away from using only externally derived evidence."

In such a coherent system where curriculum, instruction, and assessment are closely aligned with one another, one finds the following:

- Good instruction that naturally incorporates assessment of understanding and good assessment that naturally provides opportunity to further instruct.

- Ongoing informal assessment of student understanding through observations, interviews, and questioning.

- A system of formal assessment—quizzes, tests, extended tasks, projects, and portfolios— that closely reflects both what has been taught and how it has been taught.

Once again, to clarify expectations and to effectively advocate for change, principals and other school leaders are urged to use practical examples in the forms of exemplary assessments and student work to communicate the essence of these changes. Figure 3–9 shows two distinctly different ways of assessing students' understanding of perimeter. One asks for merely an answer and tells us little about understanding. The other looks for a solution and seeks to determine the depth of students' understanding *in addition to* an answer.

When students correctly answer the traditional questions, one is left wondering what they really understand. Do they merely know that perimeter means "add up all the numbers around" or do they have an understanding that the perimeter of a figure is the distance around the outside of the figure? And even worse, when students incorrectly answer the traditional questions, do they truly have a misunderstanding of perimeter or have they made a minor computation error or merely confused the words *area* and *perimeter*? None of these questions needs to be asked when examining student work on the alternative task. Notice too that the alternative task links the concept of perimeter to the idea of border and assesses only an understanding of the vocabulary ("then find the perimeter of your card") *after* the basic conceptual understanding is established. In addition, note that the alternative task calls on students to perform (design and draw) as well as to use tools (ruler) and materials (string or ribbon), thereby giving more students access to the task and a better opportunity to demonstrate what they know and can do.

These issues of assessing the depth of understanding and ensuring an alignment between how mathematics is taught and how it is assessed are evident in Figure 3–10, where a traditional exercise-like problem with one correct answer is compared with an alternative performance task with multiple solutions and numerous opportunities to assess real understanding of the concept of percent in a realistic context. Notice that the ability to correctly complete the traditional task does *not* imply the ability to correctly solve the performance task. However, students who correctly solve the performance task must demonstrate the skills required for the traditional task and so much more.

Figure 3–9   *Assessing an understanding of perimeter*

TRADITIONAL (EASY):	TRADITIONAL (HARDER):
Find the perimeter of this rectangle:	Find the perimeter of this rectangle:

Find the perimeter of this rectangle:

```
        6
   ┌─────────┐
 4 │         │ 4
   └─────────┘
        6
```

Find the perimeter of this rectangle:

```
       6
  ┌───────┐
4 │       │
  │       │
  └───────┘
```

ALTERNATIVE:

You have 20 cm of ribbon. Use your ruler to design and draw a rectangular card that uses all the ribbon as a border. Then identify the length of each side of the card and the perimeter of your card.

Figure 3–10   *Assessing an understanding of percentage*

TRADITIONAL:

What is the cost of a $50 sweater that is on sale at 25% off?

ALTERNATIVE:

At a department store sale, you are buying a $50 sweater that you selected from a table that says "25% OFF."
You also have a coupon for an additional 10% off on any purchase.

For example:

Regular price:	$60.00
Less the original 25% discount:	$45.00
Less an additional 10% discount	$39.00

> Sunday, December 23, 10–5
> Take an additional
> **10% OFF EVERYTHING**
> in the store*

The cashier takes 25% off the original $50 price and then takes an additional 10% off. She asks you for $33.75. Write what you would explain to the cashier to justify why this price is not as good as the bargain in the coupon.

Figure 3–11 is an actual third-grade test item from the spring 2007 math assessment administered in Hong Kong. Note the reasoning about volumes and conservation of volume that is assessed here. Note, too, how easy it would be to convert this to an open-ended, computer-delivered constructed-response item where students could click and drag the containers or their labels into the correct places to show the size order.

Figure 3–11   *Third-grade test item*

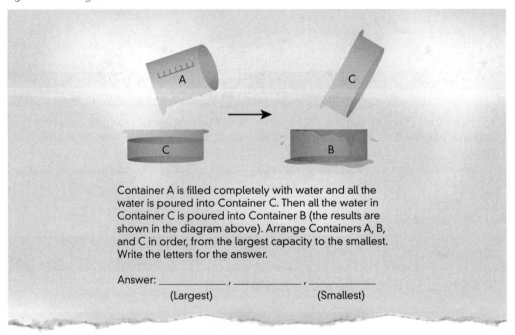

Container A is filled completely with water and all the water is poured into Container C. Then all the water in Container C is poured into Container B (the results are shown in the diagram above). Arrange Containers A, B, and C in order, from the largest capacity to the smallest. Write the letters for the answer.

Answer: _____ , _____ , _____
    (Largest)   (Smallest)

The "What's on the Test" Strategy

One approach that teachers and administrators can use to examine current assessment practices is to gather recently administered mathematics tests that teachers have given to their students. This is an effective and straightforward approach for examining whether and to what degree the assessment tools match the goals being professed. Since what we actually put on our tests and expect students to do best communicates what we deem to be important, a collection of tests gives unequaled insight into what is indeed valued in practice. So consider organizing faculty, grade-level, or department meetings around discussion of what appears on the mathematics tests given during, for example, the past two months. Among the questions one can ask about these tests are the following:

- What is the balance between short-answer questions and constructed-response questions where students must show their work and explain their reasoning?

- What aspects of the curriculum needed simply to be memorized for students to do well on these tests?
- What aspects of the curriculum needed to be well understood for students to do well on these tests?
- What, if any, are the contexts used to engage students' interest in these tests?
- What can be inferred about the methods of instruction that preceded the test?

PROFESSIONAL DEVELOPMENT SHIFTS

It's becoming increasingly common to hear that "professional development doesn't work." Certainly, serious questions about the impact of typical, and even well-designed, professional development have emerged on the basis of several recent large-scale studies of the impact of professional development funded by the Institute for Educational Studies. However, professional development, like the very K–12 instruction it is designed to improve, appears to work under some conditions and not work under other conditions. Just as instruction "works" in some classrooms and falls far short of expectations in others, so it is with professional development. While large-scale, "let's-herd-them-into-a-workshop" modes of professional development do not appear to have much, if any, impact on teacher knowledge, teacher practice, or student achievement, particular schools, particular conditions, and particular characteristics appear to be associated with positive impact on knowledge, practice, and student outcomes.

We know what is typical and does not appear to work.

- One-shot after-school workshops
- Too much passive listening to presentation rather than active learning and collaborative problem solving
- Too much focus on general topics (e.g., classroom management) rather than the specific content of the curriculum
- Too much focus on topics that have little relation to real teaching and learning needs— that is, the tasks, the instruction, and the student work that represent the heart of teaching
- Too little focus on topics that are related to students' specific learning needs
- Too much individual work rather than collegial activities by school or department
- Too little attention to follow-up, practice, and feedback
- Too little recognition that changing behavior is a long-term process

We also are well aware of the obstacles to change and improvement.

- Rarely enough time allocated to the process
- Near impossibility for change and improvement in an environment of isolation

- Limited knowledge base and opportunity to envision alternative practice
- Forces of fear, discomfort, and unwillingness to change
- A lack of confidence, insufficient support, or any real incentive to change
- The omnipresent beliefs and mind-sets that conflict with proposed changes
- Rarely any accountability for failing to change or any recognition of accomplishment

However, we have site-specific case-study and anecdotal evidence of what does appear to work.

- Teachers' development and interaction are situated in practice and built around samples of authentic work.
- Teachers' development and interaction use materials (lesson plans, records of practice, videotapes, student work, etc.) taken from real classrooms.
- Teachers' development and interaction includes frequent opportunities for:
  - collaborative and constructive feedback,
  - critique,
  - inquiry, and
  - improvement based on the observations of practice and student work.
- Teachers' development and interaction focus on the "work of teaching" and are drawn from mathematical tasks, episodes of teaching, and illuminations of students' thinking.
- Teachers assume and act on the mind-sets that
  - We're all in this together;
  - People can't do what they can't envision and won't do what they don't understand;
  - No single teacher can know it all, and we must take advantage of the knowledge and experiences of colleagues to support our individual growth; and
  - Professional sharing is part of the job, and professional growth is a core aspect of being a professional.
- Teachers' work and accomplishments are made transparent within a culture of shared accountability for success.

Chapter 6 will examine a range of strategies for making these professional development shifts in the context of professional learning communities that school leaders are responsible for instigating, orchestrating, and supporting.

TWO FORMS OF COHERENCE

Finally, when advocating for these changes in curriculum, instruction, and assessment, it is imperative that principals and other school leaders are aware of the systemic coherence that emerges from the two distinct sets of assumptions we are dealing with. So, in the tried and true "if-then" logic of the mathematician, let me summarize the implications that arise from a traditional view and from a more reformist view.

If one believes that

- mathematical skills are the primary component of a mathematics program;
- mathematical competence is not expected of all students; and
- mathematics is an appropriate social and economic sorter of humanity,

then it follows that

- a rigid system of tracking would be instituted;
- students would be denied access to more advanced levels of study;
- one would value teaching that took the form of telling and showing;
- applications would only be included *after* skills had been developed;
- technology would be approached with great caution; and
- multiple-choice tests and a focus on the right answer would predominate classroom expectations.

If, however, one believes that

- mathematics is appropriate and necessary for all students;
- problem solving and applications are the primary goals of the mathematics program; and
- mathematics is a social and economic empowerer,

then, we would expect that

- there would be less sorting and tracking of students;
- all students would be expected to study algebra, geometry, and such elements of calculus as the concept of a limit, of the derivative as a rate of change, and the integral as a summation;
- more group work during class would be evident as students collaborate;
- teachers would rely less on lecture;
- there would be less emphasis on skills, and more reliance on technology;
- students would regularly be confronted with the question "why?";
- students would be challenged to suggest alternative approaches and different solutions; and
- performance tasks, scored holistically, would take the place of short-answer, percentage-correct tests.

How do these different forms of coherence play out in real classrooms? Figure 3–12 is an effort to clarify the extraordinary differences between the traditional show-tell-practice approach and the engage-discover-connect-apply approach to teaching mathematics. It is difficult to understand how any caring parent or citizen would opt for the limited success that the traditional approach has achieved over the excitement and understanding forged by the alternative approach described previously. Ask yourself whether you really believe that subjecting twenty-first-century students to the regurgitation of procedures to arrive at correct answers could possibly prepare them for the world we currently inhabit, let alone the one that is emerging. Then, ask yourself whether the search for solutions and focus on explanations that characterize the alternative approach could possibly do harm.

It is important to recognize that the magnitude of the reform being advocated entails a major reform of the entire system. Fine-tuning only one or two aspects of the system tends to create incompatibilities that short-circuit the program and leave teachers and students frustrated. More on this subject of the components of a coherent program is presented in Chapter 7.

In summary, if we continue to do what we've always done, it shouldn't be surprising that we'll continue to get what we've always gotten. However, if what we've always gotten is no longer good enough, then the same logic that mathematicians are often so proud to rely on suggests fairly strongly that we've got to change what we've always done. At its core, this means a set of curriculum, instructional, and assessment shifts that give us a real shot at getting a lot more and lot better than we've always gotten. Anything less shortchanges students, undermines fairness, and jeopardizes our future.

Figure 3–12   *A comparison of the traditional and alternative approaches*

THE TRADITIONAL APPROACH:

The teacher informs students that today's lesson will focus on finding the volume of right circular cylinders. The teacher directs students to open their books to the appropriate page and then draws on the board: (1) a picture of a right circular cylinder very similar to one pictured in the book, and (2) the formula $V = \pi r^2 h$. The teacher then places numbers on the diagram (usually without units) for the cylinder's radius and height and proceeds to calculate the volume by plugging in the values for r and h into the formula. When the volume is calculated and students are given the chance to ask questions, the teacher assigns two practice problems that are essentially the same as the one done on the board that students can work on individually, in preparation for their homework assignment, which includes five similar problems and two applications. In such a manner, a large proportion of mathematics is "taught," regurgitated back on a quiz, and quickly forgotten.

AN ALTERNATIVE APPROACH:

The teacher begins class by holding up an empty soda can and asks students to work in pairs to find five mathematically appropriate ways of answering the question: About how big is this can?

After a few minutes, the teacher asks for, and records on the board, the various answers that students propose (for example, about 5 inches high, about 10 cm across or in diameter, about 9 inches around, about 25 cubic inches, about 300 mL, etc.). The teacher then asks each proposer to use a ruler to try to convince the class—using the actual can—that his or her estimate is reasonable.

The teacher leads the discussion toward the fact that it is often important to know (or be able to figure out) the "volume" of a container—that is, the amount of space inside the container. Often this can be connected to previous work on volume and the fact that volume has already been seen as the "area of the base times the height." This discussion and the previous student contributions should help the class to deduce the formula for calculating the exact volume of the soda can, which in turn can be validated by the capacity of 355 mL noted on the can.

To practice and reinforce these new understandings, students, working in pairs, are asked to calculate the volume of selected, found, or distributed cylinders (for example, a pencil, a CD, other cans, barrels, etc.) and report their findings to the class.

Homework is then drawn from the *Guinness Book of World Records* from which students calculate the volume of such records as the world's largest cookie, the world record for pancake consumption, or the world's largest noodle, and then connect that volume with a familiar object to provide some sense of the magnitude of the record.

4

Building Sensible, Sense-Making Mathematics
What to Encourage and Implement

One way to characterize an appropriate response to the changes described in Chapter 2 and the shifts described in Chapter 3 is as *sensible, sense-making mathematics*. Sensible mathematics is mathematics that is reasonable and rational in a technologically driven world. For example, understanding and knowing when and why to use the operation of division is sensible mathematics. However, being able to perform long division with three- and four-digit decimal divisors is no longer sensible mathematics. Sense-making mathematics is the teaching and learning of rules, procedures, techniques, and concepts in ways that make sense to students—that is, mathematics that "feels right" and "fits together" because students have been given multiple and diverse opportunities to develop understanding, not just one right way to get a single correct answer. For example, merely showing students the rules for calculating the three cases of percent (what is $x\%$ of y, x is what percent of y, and $x\%$ of what is y) is not sense-making mathematics. However, developing a clear understanding of percents as ratios to 100 and being able to represent all percent problems as proportions or equations based on scale factors or graphically as double bars are sensible mathematics.

I believe that there are ten critical characteristics of sensible, sense-making mathematics.

1. **Access**: Sensible, sense-making mathematics is taught in an environment that gives all students access to rich mathematics and invites them to learn.

2. **Alternatives**: Sensible, sense-making mathematics is taught in ways that use alternative approaches and multiple representations to develop understanding among students with diverse learning styles.

3. **Skills**: Sensible, sense-making mathematics acknowledges that although there is a rational set of skills that all students need to master, some of the skills once considered essential are today obsolete and must be purged from the curriculum. At the same time, there are skills, such as evaluating the reasonableness of an answer, that have increased in importance in an age of calculators.

4. **Concepts and big ideas:** Sensible, sense-making mathematics focuses on the development of conceptual understanding of the big ideas of mathematics that enable students to make connections and apply what they learn.

5. **Tasks**: Sensible, sense-making mathematics makes extensive use of high-quality instructional and assessment tasks to introduce, develop, reinforce, connect, apply, and assess understanding of key mathematical concepts.

6. **Language**: Sensible, sense-making mathematics relies on extensive use of language — both oral and written — to support the development of mathematical understanding in language-rich classrooms.

7. **Integration and connections**: Sensible, sense-making mathematics is taught in ways that consistently connect the mathematics being learned to familiar contexts, to other mathematical ideas, as well as to other disciplines.

8. **Alignment:** Sensible, sense-making mathematics is part of an aligned program where the curriculum, the instruction, the materials, the assessments, and the professional development are all aligned with one another.

9. **Coherence**: Sensible, sense-making mathematics is taught within coherent programs where research-affirmed learning progressions, a focus on sense making, and attention to connections within mathematics all help the pieces of the curriculum fit together in ways to support learning.

10. **Thinking and reasoning**: Sensible, sense-making mathematics is part of a thinking curriculum, as opposed to a parroting curriculum, in which "Why?" and "How do you know?" are pervasive questions in all teacher-student and student-student interchanges.

This chapter describes what each of these characteristics looks like in practice so that principals and other school leaders can encourage people to think about and implement each of these aspects of a high-quality mathematics program.

ACCESS

I often visualize the ideal mathematics curriculum as an incredibly delicious smorgasbord laid out on a beautifully decorated table. However, it doesn't take many conversations about mathematics to quickly learn that, for many, this same smorgasbord is a noxious, rotting, unappealing array of horribly distasteful stuff. The perceived unpleasantness of the mathematics table begins to emerge as early as second grade for many students. That is when the "one right regrouping approach" to get the "one right answer" for subtraction with regrouping worksheets brings sense-making mathematics to a screeching halt.

Instead of contributing to this acquired aversion, curriculum and instruction must invite students at all levels to the wonderful world of mathematics by providing intellectual, emotional, and social access to the mathematics. Four tried and true approaches to providing access—in a sense, luring students to the table of mathematics—are

- Putting the mathematics into relevant and interesting *contexts*;
- Encouraging the use of *technology* to remove the tedium from certain traditional aspects of mathematics and to enhance the display and presentation of mathematical ideas;
- Allowing students to *collaborate* as they explore mathematics; and
- Making full use of physical *materials* whenever hands-on experiences can concretize mathematics.

What is most important about these elements of access is that none of them "teach" mathematics by themselves. Students do not learn more mathematics because the problems are situated in a fast-food restaurant or because they all have powerful calculators or because they are placed in small groups with lots of manipulatives. Instead, the combination of a fast-food restaurant menu, calculators, small-group work, and concrete materials all give different students a reason to care and a structure in which they can best learn.

Figures 4–1, 4–2, and 4–3 show elementary, middle, and high school tasks, respectively, that employ everyday contexts, expect that students will be using calculators, and are well suited for cooperative learning settings. In addition to the rich and important

Figure 4–1 *Traditional and alternative elementary school problems*

TRADITIONAL:	ALTERNATIVE:
Solve the following problems:	Your class does some research and finds out that
➤ What is the cost of 5 cans of beans if each can costs $0.79?	➤ Hot dogs come in packages of 8 hot dogs for $2.50.
➤ What is the cost of 16 boxes of cereal if each box costs $2.69?	➤ Hot dog rolls come in packages of 6 for $0.90 and 12 for $1.50.
➤ How much change will Alfred get if he pays for 8 pounds of chicken that costs $1.89 per pound with a $20 bill?	➤ Hamburgers come in packages of 8 patties for $4.00.
➤ How many boxes of rice, each costing $1.59, can Sasha purchase if she has one $10 bill?	➤ Hamburger buns come in packages of 8 for $1.00 and 12 for $1.65.
	You expect that 24 students and 6 adults will come to the picnic you are planning. You also expect that most—but not all—students will have a hot dog and most of the adults will have a hamburger.
	Decide how many packages of each you should buy and find the cost of the food. Then explain your thinking and show how you arrived at the cost.

Figure 4–2   *Traditional and alternative middle school problems*

TRADITIONAL:	ALTERNATIVE:
Solve the following problems: **1.** If a man runs 5 miles per hour, how many feet per second does he run? **2.** Find the product: 2¾ × 5 = **3.** Find the volume of a right circular cylinder with a height of 15 inches and a diameter of 4 inches.	**THE WORLD RECORD FOR PANCAKE CONSUMPTION!!!** In 1977, Peter Dowdeswell of London, England, set a world record for pancake consumption! **1.** What additional information would you like to know? (How many? How big? How long did it take?) The record is 62 pancakes, each 6 inches in diameter and ⅜ of an inch thick with butter and syrup consumed in 6 minutes 58.5 seconds! **2.** Show with your hands how high a stack this would be. **3.** Exactly how high a stack would this be? (Why would the actual height of the stack probably be less?) **4.** About how fast are the pancakes consumed? (Pancakes per minute? Pancakes per second?) **5.** What is the volume of the pancakes consumed? (Is this more or less than a cubic foot?) **6.** If the average human stomach is only about 125 cubic inches, how did Peter Dowdeswell set the record? **7.** What would the radius of a single ⅜-inch-thick pancake have to be to contain the same volume as the stack that Dowdeswell consumed? **8.** Draw a graph that shows what you think Dowdeswell's progress might have looked like as he set the record. (How should the axes be labeled and what scale should be used?)

Figure 4–3   *Traditional and alternative high school problems*

TRADITIONAL:	ALTERNATIVE:
Solve for x: $3(1 + x)^{80} = 43$	In 1931, first-class postage was 3¢ for the first ounce. In 2011, first-class postage was 43¢ for the first ounce. Describe the magnitude of the increase in the cost of first-class postage between 1931 and 2011 in four different ways. Be sure that at least one of the ways includes a percent and another includes an annual compounded growth rate. Explain or show how you arrived at each way of describing the increase.

mathematics embedded in each of these tasks, each has the potential to effectively invite students into the world of mathematics and, by its very nature, forestalls the common "When are we ever going to need this?" question. It is critical that all who question the need for, or value of, a significantly reformed mathematics program consider the qualitative differences between a mathematics of practicing multiplication and division and the mathematics that arises when ordering sufficient food for a picnic; or between a page of decontextualized measurement problems and the series of questions that arise from the world record for pancake consumption; or between the rules for using logarithms to solve an exponential equation and the insights garnered from an investigation of the increase in first-class postage rates. One approach leaves far too many choking on bones and enduring a bitter aftertaste for years; the other gives students a reason to begin engaging with mathematical ideas. It's a no-brainer which approach entrenches the status quo and which approach recognizes that the Nintendo generation needs to be treated differently.

ALTERNATIVES

One of the most terrifying realities all teachers face is the fact that at any given moment, in any given class, it's very likely that more than half of our students are failing to either understand or process the mathematics being taught in the same way that that their teachers are presenting it. Call it learning styles or alternative modes of learning, it comes down to different brains working in different ways, and this phenomenon is the heart of calls for more differentiated learning opportunities. When students are asked to visualize "one quarter," one sees one-fourth of a pizza pie shaded, and another sees only the numbers one over four. Another student sees a quarter with George Washington on one side and an eagle on the other. Still another is far more comfortable with the small mark on his or her ruler one-fourth the distance between 0 and 1, and yet another sees the mark on a measuring cup between 0 and ½.

Similarly, while we may be perfectly comfortable with the symbolic abstraction of a linear function ($f(x) = 3x + 5$), some of our students need the spreadsheet or tabular representation of the same function and still others need the line that represents the function on the coordinate plane for the function to have meaning.

Just think how often teachers think or say: "They just don't get it!" That's why effective teachers never rely on the one right way to do a problem. That's why effective teachers encourage alternative approaches and employ multiple representations of key concepts to broaden the likelihood of understanding—even approaches and representations with which they themselves are not comfortable. Figure 4–4 conveys the richness of learning when teachers encourage students to come up with alternative approaches and then use the different examples of student work to help develop a stronger understanding of the connections among diverse mathematical representations. The problem in Figure 4–4 also demonstrates that even when students are given a rather insipid and

Figure 4–4 *Seven alternative solutions to the same problem*

PARTY FAVORS

Sandra is interested in buying party favors for the friends she is inviting to her birthday party. The price of the fancy straws she wants is 12 cents for 20 straws. The storekeeper is willing to split a bundle of straws for her. She wants 35 straws. How much will they cost?

SOLUTION 1:

xxxxx xxxxx—6¢

xxxxx xxxxx—6¢

xxxxx xxxxx—6¢   I drew a picture and found that the straws will cost 21 cents.

xxxxx—3¢

SOLUTION 2:

MONEY	STRAWS
3¢	5
6¢	10
9¢	15
12¢	20
15¢	25
18¢	30
21¢	35

I solved it by making a table.

SOLUTION 3:

I thought 20 ÷ 4 = 5 and 12 ÷ 4 = 3 so 5 straws for 3¢.

7 groups of 5 will cost 21¢.

SOLUTION 4:

Since 20 straws cost 12¢, you can get 10 straws for 6¢ and 5 for 3¢.

So since 20 + 10 + 5 is 35, it will cost 12 + 6 + 3 or 21¢.

SOLUTION 5:

One bundle has 20 straws. You want 35, or 15 more straws.

15 straws is ¾ of a bundle, so they will cost ¾ of 12 or 9¢.

All 35 will then cost 12 + 9 or 21¢.

SOLUTION 6:

12 is to 20 as x is to 35. Cross multiply (12 × 35) and divide by 20.

So 420 ÷ 20 = 21 and the straws will cost 21¢.

SOLUTION 7:

If 20 straws cost 12¢, each straw will cost 12 ÷ 20 or 6¢ per straw

35 straws times 6¢ per straw = 21¢.

thoroughly unreasonable problem, there is still ample opportunity for great instruction if discussion moves beyond the correct answer and toward alternative approaches.

Consider how discussions that focus on alternative approaches and multiple representations (e.g., a written explanation, a table, a proportion, or a picture) can foster better understanding and help broaden teachers' repertoire of strategies.

One of the key reasons why a focus on alternative approaches and different representations is so important is that they are the heart of effective interventions for students who need additional time, more focused instruction, or more personalized instruction to "get the math." Interventions that simply place a student in front of a computer to practice problematic skills without any attention to why the processes work, what mistakes are being made, or any human interaction are unlikely to help. Rather, successful interventions should begin with an understanding that those students who are falling behind probably need instruction that is very different from "one right way to get the one right answer" approaches—that is, interventions that focus on conceptual understanding and are replete with opportunities to use alternative approaches and different representations.

Another aspect of alternatives that we all recognize, but seldom talk about, is how rare it is to teach a perfect class and how common it is to make mistakes. In fact, we know that it is almost impossible to teach even a single forty-five-minute class without making at least two mistakes. Usually, one mistake is mathematical and careless because we're thinking two steps ahead. Sometimes our students catch our mistakes and sometimes the errors sit on the board unnoticed until no one agrees with the final answer. The second mistake is usually pedagogical and results from calling on the wrong student at the wrong time or assigning the wrong problem at the wrong time, engendering far more confusion than we'd prefer.

To make this worse, we've learned that when a principal or supervisor is in the room, we are significantly more likely to make additional mistakes. And if we're using technology, it's almost impossible to avoid hitting the wrong key at least once! Yet mistakes are often how we all best learn. They prepare us for a world that regularly expects people to "debug" situations, and they force us to reanalyze our thinking. If understanding is the goal of all learning, then focusing on alternative approaches, creating multiple representations, and debugging mistakes and errors are three powerful instructional tools for enhancing the opportunity to learn mathematics.

SKILLS

A large proportion of the controversy surrounding the reform and improvement of mathematics programs, and what is essential to teach and learn, centers on skills. What is clear is that some skills are as important, if not more important, than ever. Other skills remain in the curriculum only because of tradition.

A brief list of essential mathematical skills is not difficult to generate. For example, few disagree that all students must have a command of one-digit number facts. Students need to be able to estimate sums, differences, products, and quotients. There is widespread agreement that using various tools to measure and being able to create graphs from data presented in tables and charts are important skills. And the list goes on. My list of the non-negotiable basic skills of mathematics for all students follows:

- Zero to 10 addition, subtraction, multiplication, and division facts
- Multiplying and dividing by 10, 100, 1000
- Finding a number 10, 100, 1000, . . . 1, .01 . . . more or less than a given whole number or decimal
- Having at least one effective method to add and subtract two two- or three-digit numbers or dollar amounts to $100.00 and to multiply and divide two- and three-digit numbers by one-digit factors or divisors
- Ordering numbers, including fractions and decimals
- Estimating sums, differences, products, quotients, percents, answers, and solutions
- Understanding and identifying when and why to add, subtract, multiply, or divide in a problem situation, that is, understand and justify which of these buttons ($+$, $-$, $\times$, $\div$) to press on a calculator to solve a problem
- Identifying and using appropriate measures, approximating measures, and making everyday measurement conversions
- Identifying and creating fraction/decimal equivalents and representations
- Estimating with percents and proportional quantities
- Identifying and describing the attributes of two- and three-dimensional shapes and objects, and describing the effect of transformations (flips, slides, turns, shrinking) of these shapes and objects
- Reading and constructing tables and graphs and drawing conclusions from them
- Using and understanding the number line and the coordinate plane
- Evaluating and using formulas
- Creating and solving equations and inequalities for variable situations

But the key here is not having basic skills for the sake of completing decontextualized exercises. Rather, the goal is ensuring that all students possess these basic skills so that they can:

- Solve everyday problems
- Communicate their understanding
- Represent and use mathematical ideas

Consider, in light of this delineation of essential basics in an age of calculators and computers, the incredible amount of time and energy still expended—by teachers and their students —on increasingly obsolete skills, that is, skills no longer valued by society.

Policy makers, parents, and test developers need to give educators permission to skip textbook pages that no longer serve a useful purpose. Among those skills that should be relegated to the scrap heap are

- pencil-and-paper multiplication problems with two-digit or larger factors (three digits by one digit should be enough);
- paper-and-pencil division problems with three-digit or larger divisors (four digits by two digits should be enough); and
- computation with fractions with unreasonable denominators like sevenths or ninths (halves, fourths, eighths; thirds and sixths; fifths and tenths should be enough).

Just as important as identifying those basic skills that must remain is the need to provide ongoing practice of these important skills. Almost no one masters something new after one or two lessons and one or two homework assignments. That's why one of the most effective strategies for fostering retention and mastery is *daily, cumulative review* at the beginning of every class. Some teachers call it warm-ups; others call it daily mini-math. Some days it's delivered orally; other days it's written on the board or shown on the overhead. But everyday it's a few quick problems to keep skills sharp. And everyday teachers present something similar to

- a *fact* of the day (e.g., 7×6);
- an *estimate* of the day (e.g., if one item costs 32¢ and another costs 29¢, about how much will it cost to buy both items?);
- a *measurement* of the day (e.g., about how many meters wide is our classroom?);
- a *place value* problem of the day (e.g., what number is 100 more than 1584?);
- a *word problem* of the day; and
- any other exercises or problems that reinforce weaker, newer, or necessary skills and concepts.

CONCEPTS AND BIG IDEAS

If skills are the building blocks of mathematical competence, concepts are the connective tissue that gives mathematics its power. While, as we have seen, adding is a skill, understanding that addition is combining, putting together, and counting on is conceptual understanding. Conceptual understanding enables students to make connections between elements of mathematical knowledge that would otherwise be retained as isolated facts. It allows students to make extensions beyond their existing knowledge, to judge the validity of mathematical statements and methods, and to create appropriate mathematical representations. For example, merely finding the length of the sides of two similar triangles is procedural knowledge, but understanding the relationship between similarity and proportionality is conceptual understanding.

Conceptual understanding is often needed to perform such critical mathematical processes as making and justifying conjectures, determining the reasonableness of solutions, and constructing models and varied representations. That is, students demonstrate conceptual understanding of mathematics when they provide evidence that they can represent and classify mathematical entities; recognize, label, and generate examples and nonexamples of concepts; use and interrelate models, diagrams, manipulatives, and other representations; and identify and apply mathematical principles.

Big mathematical ideas are large, unifying concepts that help to link smaller pieces of mathematics knowledge, undergird procedural skills, and/or connect mathematics within and between content domains. They provide a key purpose for learning mathematics and serve as organizing ideas for instruction. My incomplete list of the big ideas of mathematics that need to form the core of the K–12 program follows:

- Number uses and representations
- Equivalent representations
- Operation meanings and interrelationships
- Estimation and reasonableness
- Proportionality
- Sample and sampling
- Likelihood
- Recursion and iteration
- Pattern
- Variable
- Function
- Change as a rate
- Shape
- Transformation
- The coordinate plane
- Measurement—attribute, unit, dimension
- Scale
- Central tendency

TASKS

As the focus of mathematics instruction shifts from skills to concepts and from exercises to problems, tasks have begun to replace examples as the building blocks of good instruction. Tasks—often referred to as *performance activities*—are used to engage students in thinking about and learning mathematical ideas. The tasks with which students are engaged provide rich opportunities for students to be active and to perform as they struggle to grasp important mathematical ideas. As described in NCTM's *Professional Standards for Teaching Mathematics*, good tasks provide students with opportunities "to reason about mathematical ideas, to make connections, and to formulate, grapple with and solve problems. Good tasks test skill development in the context of problem solving, are accessible to students, and promote communication about mathematics."

I have found it useful to conceptualize powerful tasks as *Performance Activities* that constitute opportunities to be *Doing Mathematics* (meaning solving problems) in *Situations* (meaning that there is a context, specific givens, and goals) for a *Purpose* (meaning that there are human goals and a definable audience). Additionally, I believe that three overarching premises help us create and adapt high-quality mathematics performance tasks.

1. Mathematics is everywhere.

2. Good mathematics arises naturally from everyday situations and data.

3. Good mathematical tasks arise in turn from the human questions that are generated by these situations and data.

Questions that mathematical skills and big ideas answer and that should be embedded in the tasks with which students are engaged are

- How much? How many?
- What size? What shape?
- How much more or less?
- How has it changed?
- Is it close? Is it reasonable?
- What's the pattern? What can I predict?
- How likely? How reliable? Is it fair?
- What's the relationship?
- How do you know? Why is that true?

In addition to stealing good tasks from textbooks and supplemental materials, good instructional and assessment tasks tend to emerge in two ways. One approach begins with data of some sort that originate in newspapers, magazines, menus, price lists, catalogs, sports, almanacs, world records, and so on. Teachers and other task developers train themselves to ask, "Where is there important mathematics in this data and what are the questions that elicit this mathematics?" A second approach begins with a chunk of mathematics that is to be taught. In this case, teachers and other task developers train themselves to ask, "When and where do normal human beings use such mathematics and how can these uses be translated into engaging tasks?"

For example, Figure 4–5 begins with a price list for difference sizes of ladders. The questions posed reveal how the data can be "mined" for tasks that deal with such mathematical ideas as unit costs, the trigonometry of ladder angles, and the algebraic modeling of determining the cost C for each ladder as a function of length L.

Regardless of the method used to develop tasks, Figure 4–6 suggests a set of characteristics for all performance tasks that emerged from Connecticut's Common Core of Learning Mathematics Assessment Project.

LANGUAGE

We often talk about mathematics as a language. Certainly, it is a language, complete with elements, notation, and syntax. A little less literally, mathematics is the language of patterns and the language of change. A little more poetically, in words attributed to Galileo, "Mathematics is the language with which God has written the universe." But more practically, language is a powerful tool for developing mathematical understanding

Figure 4–5 *How to "mine" tasks from everyday data*

LADDER PRICING

The Sunday newspaper circulars included the following chart in a hardware store flyer's advertisement for ladders:

Size	Cost
16′	$36
20′	$58
24′	$75
28′	$99
32′	$130

1. Calculate the unit price for each ladder and explain why you think the unit price changes as it does.

2. Suppose that there was demand for a 22-foot ladder. Propose an appropriate cost for such a ladder and explain how you arrived at your proposal.

3. Suppose that the top of the highest window on a house is 18 feet above ground level and that for safety reasons all ladders should be placed at an angle no greater than 75° with the ground. Which of the five ladders would be most appropriate for you to purchase? Explain how you arrived at your decision.

4. It is obvious from the chart that the longer the ladder, the more costly the ladder. Find a relationship between, or a formula that links, the length of the ladder in feet and the cost of the ladder in dollars that could be used to arrive at a price for all lengths of ladders. Build a convincing argument that your relationship or formula is appropriate.

Figure 4–6   *Characteristics of high-quality performance tasks*

Essential (not tangential): a focus on "big ideas"

Authentic (not contrived): directly involves meaningful uses of mathematics, not artificially contrived

Equitable (not biased): gives diverse students access; mathematics not hidden behind culturally exclusive information

Rich (not simplistic): numerous possibilities and solution paths lead naturally to other questions and problems

Engaging (not uninteresting): thought-provoking; fosters persistence

Active (not passive): student is worker and decision maker; student interacts with other students

Accessible (not inaccessible): a context that is inviting; students with diverse abilities and backgrounds can work actively and productively

and often a serious stumbling block for English language learners. When students articulate their answers or explain their reasoning orally, or when they show their work and "write up" their conclusions, they are using language to develop and demonstrate understanding. In fact, it is nearly impossible to teach mathematics to students who cannot read, and it extremely difficult to assess the mathematical understanding of students who cannot speak or write. This is why the importance of communication—oral and written—and discourse—between student and teacher, and among students—have become common components of improving mathematics programs. And this is why the call for interactive, language-rich classrooms is so compelling, again, especially for English language learners.

Several pieces of student work that capture these ideas are presented in Chapter 5. For now, however, Figures 4–7 and 4–8 model the use of oral and written language, respectively, and demonstrate again the difference between a language-poor, correct-answer approach and a language-rich, thinking and probing approach.

INTEGRATION AND CONNECTIONS

When a program is integrated, the mathematics being taught and learned is connected not only to other mathematics previously taught or to be taught in the future but also to other disciplines or to real-life experiences. Integrating mathematics, within mathematics, with other subject areas, and with the real world, is one of the most difficult aspects of reform. However, to ignore these connections isolates mathematics in ways that it is almost never isolated in the real world outside of school.

Figure 4–7   *Language-poor and language-rich oral approaches*

TRADITIONAL APPROACH:	ALTERNATIVE APPROACH:
Find the difference: 82 − 48	For the number sentence: 82 − 48 = *n* **1.** Make up a problem using realistic data and a common situation that would require someone to find this difference. **2.** What is a reasonable estimate for a solution to your problem? **3.** Explain how you arrived at your estimate. **4.** What is the exact answer to your problem? **5.** Explain how you arrived at this answer. **6.** After we share solutions, explain a different approach a classmate used to solve this problem.

Figure 4–8   *Language-poor and language-rich written approaches*

TRADITIONAL	ALTERNATIVE
If the average 18-year-old is reported to have witnessed 40,000 made-for-TV murders, how many murders does the average American child witness each day?	Following the spate of violent acts in schools, the president announced that "the typical American child has witnessed 40,000 murders on TV by the time he or she is 18." Survey your classmates and gather whatever data you believe is necessary to assess the reasonableness of the president's claim. Then write a letter to the president explaining how your investigation affirms or rebuts his claim.

Among the strategies for increasing the links within mathematics and between subject areas are focusing on alternative approaches and relying on interesting contexts, both of which were discussed earlier in this chapter. Figures 4–9, 4–10, and 4–11 provide three relatively straightforward situations that naturally open the door to connections with other areas of study while still providing rich opportunities to do mathematics.

ALIGNMENT

Little is more demoralizing than when teachers must confront high-stakes tests that do not match the instructional materials that are available and in use. Little is more frustrating than having to cope with a series of mixed messages about one's responsibilities as teachers and endure a litany of often conflicting directives to "follow the curriculum," "follow the pacing guide," "use the textbook," and "focus on what is tested." Little is more unprofessional than forcing teachers to participate in professional development on topics that do not relate to their jobs and with tools that are not yet available when

Figure 4–9   *Integrating mathematics and geography*

STIMULUS:

2010 Population by Continent

North America	344,529,000
Latin America and Caribbean	474,000,000
Europe	738,199,000
Asia	4,164,252,000
Africa	1,022,234,000
Oceania	36,593,000

Source: http://unstats.un.org/unsd/demographic/products/vitstats/serATab1.pdf

NONMATHEMATICAL CONNECTIONS:

1. Where are these continents located on the globe?

2. Are there any continents missing from this list? Why?

3. What do the most populous continents have in common?

MATHEMATICAL POSSIBILITIES:

1. Order the continents by population.

2. What fractional part of the world's total population resides in each continent?

Figure 4–10   *Monetary problem integrating vocabulary, history, current events, and mathematics*

STIMULUS:

A *USA Today* snippet announcing that a new $100 bill with a bigger, offset picture of Benjamin Franklin and several innovations to thwart counterfeiting goes into circulation today. So far $80 billion worth has been printed, equal to about ⅔ of all old $100 bills in use.

NONMATHEMATICAL CONNECTIONS:

1. Vocabulary: *offset, innovation, thwart, counterfeiting*

2. Who is Benjamin Franklin? Why is he pictured on the $100 bill?

3. What other bill has the picture of someone who never served as president?

4. Why do you think the government is changing the design of our currency?

5. What other contexts are there for "circulation"? What does it mean for money to circulate?

MATHEMATICAL POSSIBILITIES:

1. How many bills are represented by the $80 billion?

2. How many $100 bills are in circulation all together?

3. How large a container would be needed to store the $80 billion worth of new bills?

Figure 4–11   *Cigarette smoking problem integrating science, expository writing, and mathematics*

STIMULUS:

Heard on NPR's *All Things Considered*: Every cigarette you smoke reduces your life by 7 minutes!

NONMATHEMATICAL CONNECTIONS:

Why is cigarette smoking harmful?

MATHEMATICAL POSSIBILITIES:

Is this claim reasonable? Convince yourself that it is.

INTERDISCIPLINARY TASK:

Use the data given by NPR about reduction in life expectancy and write what you believe would be a compelling advertisement that might convince teenagers not to smoke.

teachers return to their classrooms. And little is more confusing to students than having to cope with disconnects between *what* they are expected to learn, *how* they are expected to learn it, and *how* this content is assessed. Yet these types of misalignment regularly permeate mathematics programs and undermine both teaching and learning.

One of the most exciting potentials of finally grounding the entire K–12 mathematics program on a *common* set of standards is the increased likelihood of much greater alignment. Moving from fifty different sets of state standards to a single set of standards makes it much more likely that publishers will develop materials aligned to this single set of standards instead of trying to serve fifty different masters with a single program. Similarly, building high-quality assessments, as is taking place by the PARCC and SBAC consortia, makes it much more likely that standards and assessments will be more closely aligned. It follows that the alignment of standards, materials, and assessments will result in a clearer focus for teacher training and professional development, thereby achieving the elusive goal of a far more aligned K–12 mathematics program.

COHERENCE

We hear often that there is "coherence" in the mathematics programs of high-performing Asian countries. We just as frequently hear that the U.S. mathematics program is aptly characterized as "incoherent." But just what does this mean in practical terms?

A coherent program is based on well-established *learning progressions* from grade to grade and/or course to course. That is, there is a logical structure to the development of mathematical ideas where not only does topic C follow from topics A and B sequentially but topic C builds upon and reinforces topics A and B. Teachers do not try to teach topic C until topics A and B are mastered. For example, counting expands to the use of numerals, which in turn expands to the gradual development of place value understandings. Place value understandings then undergird the development of whole-number estimation and algorithmic skills on one branch and the development of decimal understandings on a second, but related, branch. Too often in the United States there has been a clear absence of consideration of these essential learning progressions in the development of grade-level standards. Fortunately, coherent learning progressions are a key feature of the Common Core State Standards for Mathematics.

A coherent program also includes a deliberate focus on the mathematical *connections* between and among skills and concepts. That is, mathematical understanding is continually being reinforced and expanded on the basis of the conceptual links between and among topics. Decimals emerge from place value and fractions; circle graphs emerge from fractional parts, angles, degrees, and percents. Too often in the United States, skills and concepts are developed chapter by isolated chapter without explicit curricular or instructional attention to the array of mathematical connections that support learning, understanding, and problem solving.

Additionally, a coherent program focuses on *sense making* as opposed to simply memorization and the regurgitation of procedures. That is, the mathematics being taught is expected to make sense to students and is taught in ways (using questioning, multiple representations, and alternative approaches) that expect students and teachers to understand *how* the mathematics they are learning or teaching makes sense. Too often in the United States, instruction devolves to "yours is not to reason why, just invert and multiply," robbing students of the opportunity to see and understand how the mathematics they are doing makes sense.

In other words, a coherent program supports effective teaching as well as higher levels of student learning. Too often in the United States, the incoherence of the typical mathematics program seriously undermines the quality of both teaching and learning mathematics.

The two forms of coherence described in Chapter 3 compared the limited coherence of the traditional approach with an alternative, more appropriate approach. It bears repeating that *if* one believes that mathematics is appropriate and necessary for all students, that problem solving and applications are the primary goals of the mathematics program, and that mathematics must be a social and economic empowerer, *then* it would follow that, in a coherent program

- there would be less sorting and tracking of students;
- all students would be expected to study algebra, geometry, and specific elements of calculus;
- more group work would be found during class as students collaborate more;
- teachers would rely less on lecture;

- one would see less emphasis on skills and more reliance on technology;

- students would regularly be confronted with the question "Why?"

- students would be challenged to suggest alternative approaches and different solutions; and

- performance tasks, scored holistically, would take the place of short-answer, percentage-correct tests.

THINKING AND REASONING

But when all is said and done, after ensuring mastery of basic literacy and mathematics skills, the most important function of schooling is the development of thinking and reasoning skills. As captured in the standards for mathematical practice, this means that students will "reason abstractly and quantitatively" and "construct viable arguments and critique the reasoning of others." One way that this is most effectively accomplished is when "Why?" "How do you know?" or "Can you explain what you did and why you did it?" become commonplace classroom mantras that support a culture of thinking and reasoning. A student who can explain his or her answer usually has a stronger understanding of mathematics than one who can't. Classrooms where students are regularly explaining how and why—in groups and in whole-class discussions—help other students learn mathematics. That's why nearly every exhibit and example in this book asks for more than a numerical answer. That's why the dominant focus on multiple-choice testing must give way to more open-ended, constructed-response assessment. And that is why one of the most beneficial practices in any classroom is monitoring how often the word *why* is uttered—not just when incorrect answers are given but when any answer is proposed.

SENSIBLE, SENSE-MAKING MATHEMATICS AND THE COMMON CORE STATE STANDARDS

It should be both clear and gratifying to see how the features of the Common Core Standards for Mathematics discussed in Chapter 1 overlap with the ten characteristics of sensible, sense-making mathematics discussed in this chapter. When standards build from learning progressions, reduce the number of standards at each grade, and more appropriately place the content, we get higher levels of access and greater coherence. When standards consistently balance attention to skills—what students need to be able to do—and concepts—what students need to be able to know—and provide examples that demonstrate the links between skills and concepts, we get a much more balanced and appropriate program. And when the vision of the aligned assessments of the Common Core becomes reality, we get a much more aligned and integrated program.

A STRATEGY FOR ELEVATING THE VISIBILITY OF THESE COMPONENTS

A department, school, or community seeking to implement sensible, sense-making mathematics programs like those described in this chapter can elevate the visibility of each of these components by incorporating attention to each of them in all discussions pertaining to the mathematics program. Whether in discussions about the curriculum, instruction, or assessment, whether as part of discussions around DVDs of teaching or student work, or whether as part of teacher evaluation or the selection of new materials, principals and other school leaders should channel people's thinking to these issues of access, alternatives, skills, concepts and big ideas, tasks, language, integration and connections, alignment, coherence, and thinking and reasoning.

5

Pulling It All Together
Glimpses of What We Should See

It's one thing to talk about transforming curriculum and instruction and about sensible, sense-making mathematics; it's quite another to put it in place and recognize when it's taking place in classrooms. So let's turn to what high-quality, CCSSM-aligned instruction looks like and feels like in the classroom. Here is what any observer of mathematics instruction should expect to see.

Classrooms are active environments—often noisy, but clearly productive and purposeful—as students converse mathematically and wrestle with ideas in the course of solving interesting problems. It is unlikely that desks are in rows or that the teacher spends a significant proportion of class time at the chalkboard. Instead, desks are likely to be clustered in groups of three, four, or five, and calculators and other appropriate materials are readily available and being used.

Teachers are likely to be found conferring with a group of students, asking probing questions to launch an activity or draw out conjectures, stimulating discussion of findings, or summarizing the big ideas and conclusions reached by different groups. There may be traditional lecture at times as teachers introduce conventions or clarify ideas and concepts, but more often, the teacher is coaching, selecting, and orchestrating tasks, setting high expectations, and encouraging high levels of thinking and reasoning.

Similarly, no longer just passive absorbers of lecture and regurgitaters of procedures, *students* clearly assume greater responsibility for their own learning. One can see students actively engaged in doing and learning mathematics—measuring, counting, graphing, modeling, generalizing, and solving. They expect to struggle at times and bask in a sense of accomplishment at others as they gradually come to see mathematics as a living discipline and a powerful set of tools and ideas, rather than merely a collection of rules that get memorized for a test and just as quickly are forgotten.

Homework assignments are rarely pages of mindless exercises, but instead are opportunities to engage students in problems that build on work done in class, that relate to students' own lives and interests, or that involve collecting data and other information that will be used in class. Similarly, *tests and quizzes* are no longer given only at the end of a unit of instruction but are embedded parts of instruction and are often replaced with projects, classwork, and homework. All this results in *grades* that are based on multiple sources of information and that reflect a more complete view of students' understanding of mathematics than the averaged performance on traditional one-shot, one-day tests.

FROM TASKS TO STUDENT WORK: ARTIFACTS OF SENSIBLE AND EFFECTIVE MATHEMATICS

Once again, however, we have resorted to words to describe the vision of a reform-based mathematics classroom. To better crystallize this vision, teachers have increasingly used student work as artifacts of sensible, sense-making mathematics. Principals and other school leaders can easily replicate this strategy. Consider the following examples that capture engaging, concept-oriented, problem-solving, driven mathematics. Each can be used to help illustrate the outcomes of sensible, sense-making mathematics. Each can also be used to stimulate teachers to craft instruction that generates similar examples.

1. Darda Cars in Annette Raphael's Class at Milton Academy in Massachusetts

When the seventh graders in Ms. Raphael's class were studying about rates, similarity, and dimensional analysis, Ms. Raphael found an advertisement claiming that Darda toy cars went 520 miles per hour (scale speed)! Not surprisingly, her students found this hard to believe. Ms. Raphael saw this as a perfect opportunity to deal with issues of scale and proportionality. Figure 5–1 shows the letter the class sent to Darda, Inc., explaining their findings, and Figure 5–2 shows the equally wonderful letter the class subsequently received from Darda with more questions than answers.

Figure 5–1   *Class letter to Darda, Inc.*

MILTON ACADEMY

Darda, Inc.
USA Dock 2/1600 Union Avenue
Baltimore, MD 21211

Dear Darda Corporation,

We are a seventh grade math class at Milton Academy and we investigated your claim that your cars go up to 520 miles per hour scaled speed. Our teacher brought two cars (item 1150) and we tested them. We had trouble in the beginning because they did not go straight, although we found long corridors to use for the testing. We had to devise tracks laid out between foam rubber and rulers.

One group found that the car went 6 feet in .9 seconds and figured out that there are 66 and 2/3 of those .9 second intervals in one minute, so therefore the care went 400 feet in one minute or 24,000 feet in one hour. We divided by 5,280 and found out that the car goes about 4.5 miles per hour. Then we measured the wheel base of our car which was 1 and ¼ inches and measured the wheel base of a Honda Accord, which we thought was fairly standard. That was 8 feet, so we decided that it was a safe assumption that the scale of your car to a real car was 8 feet to 1 and ¼ inches or 77 to one. We multiplied the 4.5 miles per hour by the 'scaling factor' of 77 and we concluded that the car goes a scaled speed of about 346.6 miles per hour. Looking at percent of error we think that this is 170 miles per hour off what you had advertised (520 miles per hour), or a margin of error of about 33%!

Our other group took a number of trial runs and averaged that the car, when speeding against a bank of lockers which was 7 feet long, took about 1.05 seconds. There are 754.28 groups of 7 feet in a mile, so that means that 754.28 x 1.05 =791.99 seconds to go one mile. That means it takes 13.19 minutes to go that one mile. 60 divided by 13.19 minutes will tell you how many miles the car can go in one hour. That group discovered that the car goes about 4.54 miles per hour. Using the same 77 to 1 ratio to account for the difference in the size of the cars, they decided that the car could travel scaled speeds of 346 miles per hour.

We were startled with how close the results were in both groups and know that although we were using good stop watches, that there were many variables which could have accounted for the discrepancy between your numbers and ours. We would like to know how you arrived at your figure. Some people hypothesized that you used a wind tunnel or just measured the speed at the first microsecond when the acceleration is at its peak. We would also like you to know how much we enjoyed using the Darda vehicles.

We are looking forward to hearing from you. Thanks for your attention.

Figure 5–2 *Darda, Inc.'s reply to the class letter*

Darda Inc., U.S.A.

1600 Union Avenue • Baltimore, Maryland 21211 • (410)-889-1023 • FAX (410)-889-0503

Dear Students:

I'm glad you enjoyed the Darda cars. A healthy scepticism of advertising claims is a good thing to have in our current culture.

Your math skills are excellent and you have clearly proven that the cars are not traveling at 520 scale miles per hour for the distance you tested them. Does this mean we are lying to you?

Did you record the maximum speed of the car or the average speed of the car? Did the conditions under which you tested your cars allow them to reach their maximum speed? What are the ideal conditions for a Darda car? (The answer is the Darda track, which should arrive at your school soon—I sent it UPS.)

Perhaps in the meantime you can consult with your science or physics teacher about your experiment and how the way you tested and measured the cars might influence the result. You might discuss:

Friction: How does it affect speed?

The difference between acceleration and speed: is the moment of maximum acceleration the same as the moment of maximum speed?

Acceleration curves—at what distance from its starting point does the Darda car reach its maximum speed?

Maximum vs. average speed.

We don't claim that no matter what you do, our cars will go 520 scale miles per hour, we claim that under their own power they can go as fast as 520 scale miles an hour.

Are we telling the truth?

Looking forward to your reply,

Larry Grubb,
Darda R&D

2. TV Viewing in Ms. Cavanaugh's Class at the Gideon Welles Middle School in Connecticut

When Ms. Cavanaugh's class was studying statistics and data analysis, she gave her class the Television Viewing Habits and Their Impact task that I had designed and shared with teachers. Figure 5–3 shows the task and one piece of work completed by students in her class.

Figure 5–3 *TV viewing habits task and student response*

As a result of an instructional program in mathematics like that described in this guide, by the end of grade 8, all students should be expected to complete work like the sample below:

TELEVISION VIEWING HABITS AND THEIR IMPACT

The following project assesses your ability to integrate and use your mathematical understandings to gather data, analyze the data and communicate your conclusions. You will have approximately two weeks to complete this project.

The following editorial appeared in your local newspaper:

> ### TV CONTINUES TO ROT YOUNG MINDS
>
> The evidence is clear. Study after study confirms what parents have suspected all along:
>
> - American children watch too many hours of TV;
> - American children watch too much violence on TV; and
> - American children watch too many hours of cartoons.
>
> One study suggests that for every hour spent in school each week the average 12-year-old watches two hours of TV! Another study suggests that the typical child has seen 10,000 made-for-TV murders by age 14! And researchers have found that, by age 10, many children have already watched almost a year of cartoons!
>
> It's time for parents to turn the TV off. It's time for children to rediscover reading and games and conversation and homework. It's time to stop the rotting of the minds of our young people.

Do you agree? Do editorials like this one make you angry? Do you believe what the studies show and the researchers mentioned in the editorial say? Well, how about doing something about it.

Your task for this project is to: Write a detailed letter to the editor that summarizes how and why you agree or disagree with the claims made in the editorial. Your letter must be supported by data you collect from other students in your class or school. This data should then be organized into graphs or charts that should be included in your letter.

(continued)

Figure 5–3   *TV viewing habits task and student response (continued)*

To successfully complete this task you are expected to:

➤ design a survey that will allow you to test the claims made in the editorial;

➤ conduct the survey and gather data from at least 30 students;

➤ analyze the data and create some graphs or charts to display the data you have collected; and

➤ write a detailed letter to the editor that summarizes your findings, includes your graphs or charts, and states clearly whether or not you agree with the claims made in the editorial and why.

Your work will be evaluated on how well you have:

➤ identified the claims and gathered data to test the claims;

➤ organized your thoughts and used your data to argue for or against a claim or claims—that is, how good a case you make in support of or against each claim;

➤ used important mathematical ideas in designing your survey and analyzing your data; and

➤ communicated your findings effectively—both in words and graphically.

————————————

May 8, XXXX

Dear Editor of the Glastonbury Citizen:

In your recent editorial about **Television Viewing Habits and Their Impact: TV Continues to Rot Young Minds**, I totally disagree with every statistic you gave to the people of Glastonbury. But I do agree with your comments that American children watch too much TV, too much violence on TV; and children watch too many hours of cartoons. In the following paragraphs I have listed statistics that are reasonable than the one originally listed.

In the article one study suggests that for every hour spent in school each week, the average 12-year-old watches 2 hour of TV. That says that this child witch spends about 8 hours in school is spending 16 hours watching TV when he or she gets home. I would like to know what kind of person this is! The calculator must have forgot that each child spends time studying, eating, and sleeping. I provide a graph to show the daily schedule of a 12-year-old.

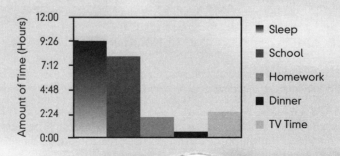

DAILY SCHEDULE FOR A 12-YEAR-OLD

(continued)

Figure 5–3   *TV viewing habits task and student response (continued)*

The time in which the child could watch TV was based on the fact that he or she would get up at 7AM and get ready for school. Then they would start school at 8AM and would then be home by about 4PM.

Once they got home, he or she could do homework, eat, or watch TV in any order for about the next 5 hours 30 minutes until they had to go to bed at 9:30 PM. Most children go to bed about that time and don't stay up later but for the ones that do I have included a couple more minutes in the graph. Maybe your stats came from aliens.

Now, I agree with the fact that American children watch too much violence on TV. But, another study in the article suggests that the typical child has seen 10,000 made-for-TV murders by age 14. I disagree with this suggestion. One factor that first has to be considered is that from age 1–3 the child will not be interested in a show without songs and lots of color like a cartoon. Second, there are about 60 made-for-TV murders per month on TV. Here are the steps I followed in order to come to my conclusion.

60 TV murders (x) 12 months (x) 11 years of watching = Amount TV murders viewed

60 x 12 x 11 = 7,920 TV murders

In this area, if you were to also include all of the murder movies your number of murders could be well over 10,000 murders. But, if you don't like the murder movies both the number of TV murders and movie murders would be lower. But the real violence comes from other shows like Mighty Morphing Power Rangers, or any other ninja or fighting shows. That should have been another study.

My final topic is I agree that American children watch too many hours of cartoons but disagree with the research that says that by the age of 10, children have already watched almost a year of cartoons. I say that they watch even more than that, it is about 1 year and 3 months! Here is how I came to my conclusion. I computed that at age 1, most babies aren't interested in cartoon. (I have a one-year-old brother.) But from age 2–7 one child watches about 4 hours of cartoons a day. So I then said it would take 6 days to make 24 hours of TV. Next, I divided 365 days by 6 and received 60.833. Last, I multiplied 60.933 by 24 then by 6, which stands for 6 years of watching cartoon.

365/6 = 60.833   60.833 x 24 = 1459.992   1459.992 x 6 = 8,759.9   about 8,760

Next, to figure out the amount of cartoons watched by children ages 8–10 first I divided 365 by 12 days in would take to complete 24 hrs. of TV. I figure at this age kids have more activities and are more interested in other programs. Then I multiplied that product by 24. At last, I multiplied that new product by 3 years of viewing.

365/12 = 30.416   30.416 x 24 = 729.984   729.984 x 3 = 2,189.952   about 2,190

2,190 + 8,760 = 10,950 hours of cartoons after 10 years of age

There are only 8,760 hours in one year, so kids see a lot of bugs and daffy duck!

In conclusion, next time you print an editorial about recent statistics, please make sure they look correct so there won't be confusion and people angry with false information.

Sincerely,

3. Ice Cream Cones in Jim Cochrane's class at Lewis Mills High School in Connecticut

Similarly, while teaching his geometry students about finding the volume of regular three-dimensional figures, Mr. Cochrane posed the following task:

THE ICE CREAM CONE

You may or may not remember that the volume of a sphere is $\frac{4}{3} \pi r^3$ and the volume of a cone is $\frac{1}{3} \pi r^2 h$. Consider the Ben and Jerry's ice cream sugar cone, 8 cm in diameter and 12 cm high, capped with an 8 cm in diameter sphere of deep, luscious, decadent, rich, triple chocolate ice cream. If the ice cream melts completely, will the cone overflow or not? Explain your reasoning and show your work.

Figure 5–4 shows the work of one student in Mr. Cochrane's class and demonstrates both a depth of understanding and a strong ability to communicate mathematically, as well as a great sense of humor.

Figure 5–4   *One student's response to the ice cream cone problem*

(continued)

Figure 5–4   *One student's response to the ice cream cone problem (continued)*

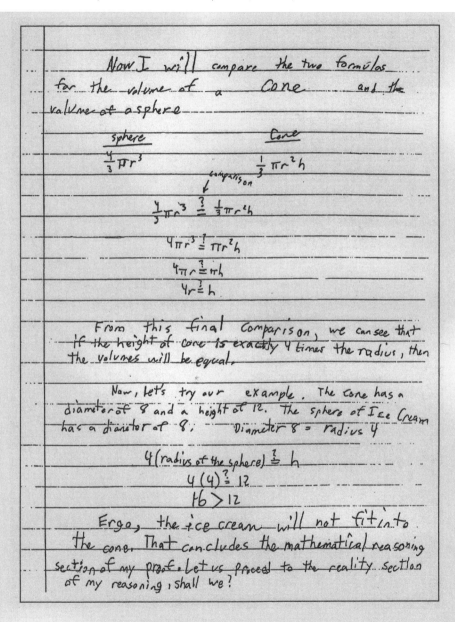

Now I will compare the two formulas for the volume of a Cone and the volume of a sphere.

sphere   Cone

$\frac{4}{3}\pi r^3$ $\frac{1}{3}\pi r^2 h$

comparison

$\frac{4}{3}\pi r^3 \stackrel{?}{=} \frac{1}{3}\pi r^2 h$

$4\pi r^3 \stackrel{?}{=} \pi r^2 h$

$4\pi r \stackrel{?}{=} \pi h$

$4r \stackrel{?}{=} h$

From this final comparison, we can see that if the height of cone is exactly 4 times the radius, then the volumes will be equal.

Now, let's try our example. The cone has a diameter of 8 and a height of 12. The sphere of Ice Cream has a diameter of 8.   Diameter 8 = radius 4

4(radius of the sphere) $\stackrel{?}{=}$ h

4(4) $\stackrel{?}{=}$ 12

16 > 12

Ergo, the ice cream will not fit into the cone. That concludes the mathematical reasoning section of my proof. Let us proceed to the reality section of my reasoning, shall we?

(continued)

Figure 5–4 *One student's response to the ice cream cone problem (continued)*

Many questions need to be answered as to how the ice cream will act in real life.

- Will the ice cream's volume change as it melts?
- Is it possible to compress ice cream?
- Is the ball of ice cream a perfect sphere?
- Is ice cream porous?
- Is the interior of the cone perfectly smooth?
- What kind of Ice cream is it?
  (bubble gum, chocolate chip, rocky road)
- Is there a hole at the tip of the cone?
- Why is the sky blue?

These questions and many more must be left unanswered. I do not poses the proper equipment or funds to do experiments with ice cream.

My hypothesis is that when the ice cream melts it will take up less space. I'm not sure if it will be small enough to fit inside the cone, however.

4. Burger King in Tom Kessell's Class at Antioch High School in Illinois

When the all-important percents unit arrived in Mr. Kessell's Transition Math class, he began the unit with a "percent scavenger hunt." Each student was asked to bring "three percents" to class—percents found on labels, in articles, in advertisements, and so on. One student arrived in class the following day with the Burger King ad that reads, "Our Hamburgers are 75% Bigger," with the fine print reading "by weight of uncooked hamburgers." Once again, students were startled by the apparent exaggeration in the claim. With Mr. Kessell's assistance and encouragement, the class conducted a detailed experiment and investigation into the actual differences in size between the Whopper and the Big Mac. Figures 5–5 and 5–6 contain the letter from the class to Burger King and the table of data. Figure 5–7 contains the response back from Burger King.

Figure 5–5 *Class letter to Burger King*

Barry J. Gibbons, CEO
Burger King
17777 Old Cutler Rd.
Miami, FL 33157

Dear Mr. Gibbons,

I am writing on behalf of my fellow students and teacher in my Transition Math class. In that class we have been working with percentage.

During a discussion, your commercial, claiming that you hamburgers have 75% more meat than those of McDonalds, came up. The discussion turned into such a frenzy that our teacher realized that we had an obvious interest in the subject.

The next day we were excited to see that our teacher had done some research. On his desk were two bags. In them were hamburgers, one cooked and uncooked from Burger King, and the same from McDonalds. As we looked we were shocked. It was hard to believe that McDonalds hamburger meat was so small compared to yours. I was one of those doubters, so that night I went and did the same. What I found was no different than what we had found in class.

The following day we did extensive testing. Weighing and measuring the two burgers. During the testing we determined that your burger was 80% bigger and not 75%. We were wondering why not just say 80%?

Our class applauds Burger King for giving the customer what they really want.

Sincere thanks,

Figure 5–6   *Table comparing Burger King data and McDonald's data*

PERCENTS IN ADVERTISING

Comparison of products

Burger King advertised that their hamburger is 75% larger than McDonald's. The advertising states that the 75% is by weight of uncooked hamburgers. The class examined one frozen and one cooked hamburger from both Burger King and McDonald's. The results are as follows:

	Cooked			**Frozen**	
McDonald's					
Diameter	3⅛ in			3⅞ in	
Thickness	¹¹⁄₃₂ in			¼ in	
Volume	2.6 cu in			2.9 cu in	
Weight	27.1 grams			43.7 grams	
Burger King		**% Increase**			**% Increase**
Diameter	3⅞ in	24%	4⅝ in		19%
Thickness	⁷⁄₁₆ in	27%	⁵⁄₁₆ in		25%
Volume	5.2 cu in	100%	5.3% cu in		83%
Weight	48.8 grams	80%	79.1 grams		81%

5. American Cheese on the Pilot New York State Assessment

Finally, when building prototype tasks for a new statewide assessment, test developers in New York State opted *not* to ask students to "Express 1¾ as a decimal." Instead, students were given the following task:

> You order 1¾ pounds of American cheese. The clerk sliced the cheese, put it on the scale, and stopped when the scale read 1.34 pounds. Explain what you would say to the clerk to be sure you get the right amount of cheese.

Consider the difference between the one-right-answer question and the more open-ended task, and consider the difference in the responses each would elicit.

A representative set of answers from one class follows:

- Turn it into a fraction.
- Wait until it says 1.75.
- 1¾ is 1.75, not 1.34 because it's 3 out of 4.
- I do not understand.
- I would say thank you, because it is the correct amount.
- Give me more, you klutz.
- Get me someone who knows what they're doing around here.

Figure 5–7   *Burger King's reply to class letter*

> JAMES ADAMSON
> CHIEF EXECUTIVE OFFICER
>
> Mr. Thomas R. Kessell
> Antioch Community High School
> 1133 Main Street
> Antioch, IL 60002-1899
>
> Dear Mr. Russell:
>
> I was delighted to receive your letter and read about the experiment your class conducted! To be the best hamburger restaurant in the world, we at Burger King have worked hard to ensure that we are serving our customers bigger, better hamburgers that are flame-broiled--not fried. As you and your students have seen, we are offering a far superior product to that of McDonald's.
>
> I have enclosed Free WHOPPER® Sandwich coupons for you and your class to enjoy. Again, thank you for writing us here at Burger King.
>
> Sincerely,
>
> James B. Adamson
>
> BURGER KING CORPORATION · 17777 OLD CUTLER ROAD · P.O. BOX 020783 · MIAMI, FLORIDA 33102-2783
> (305) 378-7770· FAX (305) 378-7403

These answers, both correct and incorrect, partial and without a clue, become a wonderful starting point for additional instruction.

These exemplars of student work and the tasks from which they emerge provide powerful models of instruction and assessment that reflect the standards for mathematical practice. They capture, for example, students making sense of problems and persevering in solving them, students reasoning abstractly and quantitatively, students constructing viable arguments and critiquing the reasoning of others, and students modeling with mathematics.

The bottom line here is that our focus must be far less on what adults say than on what students actually do. The tasks and the student work that they have elicited, as presented in this chapter, are the clearest indicator of whether mathematics instruction is or is not working, is or is not sensible, and is or is not resulting in student learning of important mathematical ideas. There can be little doubt that the classes in which this work was produced are representative of mathematics classes we would hope to see for all students.

6

Recognizing and Overcoming Obstacles
Insights and Practical Strategies

As was noted in the introduction, people cannot do what they cannot *envision*. People will not do what they don't *believe* is possible or can work. People will not implement what they do not *understand*. People are unlikely to do well what they don't *practice*. People who practice without *feedback* don't progress efficiently. People who work without *collaboration* are unlikely to sustain their effort. These truisms of human nature and organizations remind us that all of the efforts to implement the changes discussed in this book must be grounded in

- creating and sharing a vision for school mathematics;

- helping people understand and embrace this vision;

- showing people that reform *is* possible and *does* work;

- providing multiple opportunities for teachers to practice, receive feedback, and collaborate; and

- building people's understanding so they become confident in their own ability to do things differently and better.

Change agents and other advocates of reform have learned that changing *behavior* requires changes in *beliefs* and in *conditions*. It also means modeling what is being advocated through demonstrations and examples. Given the magnitude of the changes we are asking teachers of mathematics to make and the obstacles these teachers face in trying to move forward, principals and other school leaders need specific strategies for providing leadership and assistance. This chapter examines some of the major obstacles to change and proposes a set of practical strategies—framed as professional learning community practices—for helping to overcome these obstacles, reduce isolation, improve conditions, inculcate a vision, change beliefs, and ultimately change behaviors.

We know that people do not grow and organizations do not change when they are isolated. The professional isolation of most educators is frequently cited as the most serious impediment to improving curriculum, instruction, and assessment. Most teachers practice their craft behind closed doors, minimally aware of what their colleagues are doing, usually unobserved and undersupported. Far too often, teachers' frames of reference are how they were taught, not how their colleagues are teaching. Common problems are too often confronted individually, rather than by seeking cooperative and collaborative solutions to shared concerns. To reduce this debilitating isolation we must make professional interaction and sharing the centerpiece of what we do. Whether peer observations, team-teaching, formal and informal opportunities for professional sharing stimulated by common readings or common problems or student work, issue-focused faculty or department meetings, action research teams, course committees, or simply common planning time, it is time to help our colleagues become dynamic communities of learners, rather than just assortments of educators working in the same school or district. We know that professional interaction—often informal and unstructured—is often far more influential than more formally organized professional development.

TEACHERS OF MATHEMATICS ARE DIFFERENT

The deep, dark secret in schools is that all teachers and all schools are *not* the same. Schools *are* different and different teachers have different strengths and different needs. In our rush to democratize our initiatives, we overlook the fact that teachers of mathematics are being asked to teach in distinctly different ways than how they themselves were taught. The magnitude of the challenge facing teachers of mathematics and, even more important, those supporting and supervising teachers of mathematics can best be seen by comparison to teachers of other disciplines.

Here's how I see it: In terms of core content, over the past thirty years, in broad oversimplification, teachers of language arts have been forced to replace one Shakespearean sonnet and one Dickens novel with a Maya Angelou poem and a more current novel like Ray Bradbury's *Fahrenheit 451* or Michael Shaara's *The Killer Angels*. But genre is still genre, plot is still plot, and literature is taught as it was in high school, as it was in college, and as it was twenty years ago. Similarly, teachers of social studies have advanced over the same twenty years from the film-strip projector to the 35mm projector to the VCR and DVD, while the Civil War and its causes haven't changed much. Compare this to teachers of mathematics who wrestle daily with what to do about long division, or how much time to spend on other skills that are no longer done with paper and pencil, or what to do about the "solve" button on a calculator that makes an agonizingly large proportion of the high school curriculum obsolete.

Although this comparison may suffer from a bit of hyperbole, the simple fact is that mathematics is different. The changes, the choices, and the decisions faced by teachers of mathematics are qualitatively different from those of teachers of other disciplines. We need to make the case that, given the differential needs, equality of professional development resources at this time is not equitable, nor is it wise if we are to meet the urgent societal and economic needs discussed earlier. It's not that teachers of mathematics are more important, it's just that the magnitude of the changes we are asking them to implement require more than just their fair share.

OBSTACLES TO CHANGE

Before examining a set of strategies to assist teachers and to scale up reform efforts, it is critical to pause and delineate the obstacles to change that the vast majority of teachers face daily.

Professional Isolation

It is unreasonable to expect teachers to implement changes on the order of what is needed when so much of their professional lives are conducted in such isolation. Teachers cannot be expected to implement the kinds of changes involving new technologies, new programs, and new approaches when they are unaware of available resources and instructional materials. Without support for ongoing professional development, opportunities to attend conferences, and access to professional journals, teachers and their supervisors remain unacceptably ignorant of the paths to change and improvement. It is inconceivable that we would be as complacent about the professional isolation of those in the medical profession. Yet the abiding sense that teachers arrive in a classroom on day one fully prepared to teach for thirty years with only minimal professional growth lingers dangerously in our culture.

Lack of Confidence and Fear of Change

It is also critical to remember that as educators, our first and foremost responsibility is to serve as perpetuators of the culture. We tend not to be radical agents of change. In fact, educators have been and continue to be hired to pass on the rich lore, traditions, and mores of the culture. And what more powerful elements of our mathematical culture exist than things like long division, the quadratic formula, and drill-and-kill worksheets? This cultural component helps explain why changing the traditional curriculum and shifting time-honored instructional practices requires a degree of self-confidence and a willingness to take risks that the teaching profession has rarely reinforced.

Fear of Failure

Like in most of life, it is often much safer and much easier to maintain the mediocrity of the status quo than it is to risk the failure that change might entail. Teachers legitimately worry that they have failed when a principal criticizes an active, cooperatively grouped classroom as "too noisy" and "insufficiently under control." Teachers legitimately worry that they have failed when, after an exciting mathematical exploration with several engaging tangents, students say, "This was fun. Do we have to do real math tomorrow?" or ask "When are we going to get to do math?" having been conditioned to think that learning mathematics consists solely of individual practice of newly presented procedures. And teachers legitimately worry that they have failed when a colleague, who now has several students whom they taught the previous year, asks why they didn't teach a particular skill that was deemed to be obsolete and omitted to make room for a new unit on, for example, data analysis. No one likes to fail, to feel in jeopardy of failing, or to be accused, albeit unfairly, of failing. So it should not be surprising that teachers often structure their behavior to avoid any real deviation from tried and true methods. There is a strong tendency to "go along to get along," even when it is obvious that "going along" isn't meeting students' needs. While "nothing ventured, nothing gained" is an apt aphorism for much of life, "nothing risked, nothing failed" is a far more powerful descriptor of what is too often done in schools.

Lack of Support

Given how scary and difficult it is to make change, it should be obvious that support is crucial for people being asked to change. All who call for change must understand that without both moral and tangible support and ongoing encouragement from colleagues and administrators, few will take, and even fewer will persist in taking, the requisite risks. Without support in the face of the misguided complaints of a few vocal parents, few teachers will change. Without support for quality professional development and time for sharing ideas and practices, little change is possible, and without the support for calculators, computers, and newer instructional materials, change is nearly impossible. Although beliefs and will are more important than money, without a reasonable financial investment—the most tangible form of support—little change is likely.

Insufficient Time

The blunt truth is that there is never enough time to do all we want to do. However, as individuals and groups of individuals we have always displayed an uncanny ability to find time for what we value and need to find time to do. Teachers, administrators, faculties, and mathematics departments will always use the excuse of insufficient time to make change. But when and where there is a will—a collegial commitment—to making change to better serve students, insufficient time no longer remains an insurmountable obstacle.

OVERCOMING THE OBSTACLES BY BUILDING AND SUPPORTING PROFESSIONAL LEARNING COMMUNITIES

The most effective and professionally happiest schools and mathematics departments I've worked with have systematically overcome these obstacles and have reduced professional isolation with an ongoing array of professional learning community activities within a culture of transparency, sharing, and mutual support. These pockets of excellence and reformed practices exist throughout the United States and are testimony to the fact that it can be done. How has this been accomplished? The answers lie in the antidotes of sharing, supporting, and risk taking forming the bedrock for enhanced professionalism. More specifically, principals and other leaders have instigated, orchestrated, and supported obstacle-overcoming initiatives like those described next.

The overarching construct for designing effective professional development for teachers of mathematics is that professional growth activities for teachers should parallel the effective instructional and assessment strategies we advocate in our Standards for students. That is

- just as students need to be actively engaged in their own learning and construct their own understanding, so too must professional development for teachers actively engage them in the process of constructing understanding of mathematics, pedagogy, and students' needs;

- just as students need time to explore, practice, refine, and apply new understandings, so too must professional development for teachers provide adequate time and support to explore, practice, discuss, refine, apply, and reflect upon new ideas, techniques, and practices;

- just as students need feedback and support from teachers and peers, so too do teachers need feedback and support from colleagues and supervisors, particularly when changes are being implemented;

- just as classrooms are the primary unit of focus for students, so too must school and department faculties be the primary unit of attention when implementing effective professional development; and

- just as student learning of mathematics is the ultimate goal of classroom instruction, so too must student learning of mathematics be the ultimate goal of all professional development.

In other words, we must model in our practices those things that we preach: What constitutes good instruction for our students is also what constitutes effective professional development for our colleagues. More specifically, we must cultivate and adopt such practices such as

Common readings and focused discussions where "communities of learners" are developed. Selected journal articles, passages from the NCTM Standards, and sections of the Common Core State Standards for Mathematics are excellent fodder for discussions that can be built around focus questions like:

- To what degree are we already addressing the issue or issues raised in this article?
- In what ways are we not addressing all or part of this issue?
- What are the reasons that we are not addressing this issue?
- What steps can we take to make improvements and narrow the gap between what we are currently doing and what we would like to do?

The articles included in the appendix all also provide excellent fodder for these focused discussions and help to engage people's beliefs and biases about mathematics instruction.

Demonstration classes and video-recorded lessons where teachers have the opportunity to see and discuss what colleagues are doing. Viewing videos of colleagues teaching or collaboratively watching a colleague teach fosters a strong sense that "we're all in this together." It often provides a sense of family when common problems are confronted with empathy and even a healthy comic relief that strengthens a mathematics department or a grade-level team of teachers. In addition, videos of everyday lessons and demonstration lessons provide invaluable insights into what is really going on in colleagues' classrooms and communicate powerfully that teachers are not alone in what they face.

Faculty seminars where teachers take control of their own professional growth. For some issues—particularly those relating to mathematical knowledge—readings, discussions, and viewing lessons are insufficient to raise the collective knowledge base of a group of teachers. For example, before plunging into graphics, calculators, or topics in discrete mathematics or algebraic thinking in elementary grades, teachers need to confront their own learning needs. Department and faculty seminars are excellent vehicles to meet these needs to know more mathematics or to learn about topics or techniques that were neither needed nor discussed ten or twenty years ago. Such seminars, organized by and for colleagues and conducted by fellow teachers or outside resource people, allow a department or a faculty to admit and address their needs. Just as a powerful camaraderie builds among students in a group that struggles together, so too do faculties build an esprit de corps through such seminars that makes learning and changing a far less threatening experience.

Faculty and department meetings where colleagues come together to share, support, and learn. Effective and professionally enriching meetings

- are conducted regularly, with notification made well in advance and with agendas published and distributed prior to the meeting;
- limit administrivia, including scheduling, inventory, ordering, grading, and so on to no more than 25 percent of the meeting;
- include reports from faculty or department members serving on school and department committees;
- systematically encourage sharing, questioning, and suggestions about issues of curriculum, instruction, and assessment;
- often include a "key topic of the meeting" featuring discussion led on a rotating basis by members of the faculty; and
- conclude with a summary of assignments for the next meeting.

Classroom visits where—like in Japan—teachers are often found in the back of classrooms observing colleagues. One of the easiest ways to reduce isolation and insulation is through school or department expectation that teachers regularly and informally visit the classrooms of their colleagues. Although such periodic visits—made during preparation times at the middle and high school levels or when students are in art, music, or physical education at the elementary level—are often uncomfortable at first, they soon become standard operating procedure as teachers come to welcome and expect constructive feedback from colleagues. Sitting in each other's classrooms, even for as little as twenty minutes, sometimes with follow-up discussions, often initiates some of the most useful collegial discussions and makes experimentation and risk taking far more likely and far easier.

Grade-level and course committees where teachers assume ownership over what they teach. In many effective mathematics programs, the critical responsibility for curricular and instructional updating is assigned to grade-level and course committees comprising teachers who daily teach in that grade or that course. Such committees, one for each grade level and major mathematics course, consist of several teachers who are charged with making annual recommendations to their colleagues regarding content additions and deletions, instructional practices and materials, and assessments—including course final exams or end-of-grade criterion-referenced tests. Grade-level and course committees are effective vehicles for institutionalizing sharing and substantive collegial interaction, as well as excellent mechanisms for giving teachers ownership over the improvement of practice.

LEADERSHIP THAT SUPPORTS GROWTH AND CHANGE

What is obvious in education, and in all other settings, is that leadership remains the critical variable for change to occur and for change to be institutionalized in schools and districts. The three leadership strategies that I have found to be significant are granting permission, validating outliers, and catching the flak.

Granting Permission

Instead of telling people what to do, an alternative strategy is giving people permission to do what you would like them to do anyway. For example, in Connecticut we decided to use the revised objectives on our state tests in mathematics to give teachers permission to limit all pencil-and-paper multiplication to one-digit factors, arguing that two- and three-digit factors are fodder only for estimation, calculators, or both. We gave similar public permission to reduce the computational load to one-digit divisors in division and limit fractional computation to reasonable denominators (as opposed to sevenths and ninths).

Similarly, I am often struck by the degree of embarrassment expressed when teachers I've observed have made minor computational errors in the midst of lessons. Again, "permission to make a few mistakes," especially if technology or manipulative materials are being used, communicates that perfection is not expected and goes a long way to encourage and support risk taking.

Leaders need to give colleagues permission to skip unnecessary lessons or even whole chapters in textbooks, permission to try new materials, permission to experiment with portfolios, permission to deviate, and permission to take risks.

Validating Outliers

Every one of us is blessed with exemplary colleagues. These are the teachers, administrators, and coworkers who are ahead of the curve. They are the people who are hard at work daily making the vision of the Standards a reality in their classes, schools, and districts. Everyone knows who these people are, and we know they are the ones who make us look good. Unfortunately, within the culture of many schools, many of these people are outliers. They are often shunned by their colleagues and they are uncertain the extra work they do and the risks they take are worth the extra time, effort, and grief. I believe that one of the critical aspects of our job is the deliberate and ongoing validation of these special outliers.

As leaders we need to encourage these people. We need to provide them with extra support and nurture them as the precious resource they are. We need to assure them that the eccentricity so often ascribed to them is a crucial and valued source of their professional competence. We need to reassure them that their time and efforts truly are appreciated. And we need provide opportunities for networking and sharing among these atypical educators.

Catching the Flak

In these times of increasingly strident backlash and increasingly angry assaults on what we do, it's natural for people to become a little gun-shy. At exactly the point when the changes recommended by the mathematics reform effort require a little risk taking, many of us encounter conditions that make it just that much harder to take these risks. Think of the wary parent taking it out on a teacher who listened to us and reduced the frequency of drill-and-practice worksheets. Or think of the frustrated guidance counselor taking it out on the teachers who listened to us and are trying to implement an algebra for all philosophy.

Leaders run interference. They "catch the flak" and protect the people on the firing line by meeting with the disgruntled parents or by helping wayward guidance counselors understand the mathematics program. Leaders intercede when administrators prevent teachers from moving ahead, and they ensure that the inevitable backlash is responded to head-on and side-by-side. In short, they assume responsibility and don't leave others holding the bag.

I have noted earlier that while "nothing ventured, nothing gained" is an apt aphorism for much of life, "nothing risked, nothing failed" is a far more powerful descriptor of what we do in schools. I believe this applies as much to leaders unwilling to take risks as it does to teachers unwilling to change.

LEADERSHIP THAT MOVES FROM DIGNITY TO ACCOUNTABILITY

Finally, it's time to recognize the folly of top-down demands for accountability in an environment where there is so little collaboration and quality, and the equivalent folly of expecting quality when there is so little dignity or transparency. Watching and reflecting upon the differences between high- and low-performing schools and departments and between energizing and enervating workplaces and professional and unprofessional environments, it is clear that the critical progression is from dignity to transparency to collaboration to quality to accountability.

Let's be honest about what is missing in so many of our schools and departments. There isn't enough *dignity* as too few are too rarely treated as professionals. There isn't enough *transparency* as too many either hide behind classroom doors or end up professionally isolated. There isn't enough *collaboration* as there is far too little professional sharing. There isn't enough *quality* as we know that much can be done much better. And there isn't much meaningful *accountability* as it is too often minimal, weak, or based on the wrong outcomes. So let's look at each of these elements in turn.

Dignity

Too often directives are top-down demands that assume those on the front lines are either ignorant, consummate slackers, or both. There is this sense that everyone knows more and better than teachers. And in far too many schools, the students are not treated any better. In other words, far too many schools forget or ignore the foundational importance of treating people with dignity and respect. Alternatively, when people are treated like the professionals they are, it's simply amazing how often they begin to act professionally. When students are treated with respect it's just as amazing how classroom and school behaviors start to improve. It's a too frequently ignored truism that dignity and respect are essential precursors to trust and a healthy work environment!

Transparency

Too often, the people in many schools I visit hide behind closed doors, hoard lest others "steal" one's ideas, rarely observe or know what their colleagues are doing, and rarely video themselves practicing their craft. This is not bad or evil behavior. It is simply the ambient culture of the school. Alternatively, consider a school in which people never know when a colleague might wander in while teaching is going on because the entire staff feels completely welcome in everyone else's classroom. Consider a school where teachers collegially review videos of their lessons and where there is schoolwide access to test results and grades. In other words, consider the chasm between a culture that borders on secrecy and a culture of transparency.

Collaboration

Way back in 1971, when I began my career as the hippie math teacher, I literally could do it all. I had three different textbooks, two walls of blackboards, a stash of chalk, boxes of ditto masters, and one overhead projector and a screen. That's all there was and that's all I needed to do my job. Who needed to collaborate? And today's array of tools? Consider the teacher of mathematics who has access to, and must plan for and juggle, textbooks, videos, websites, assorted applets, an amazing array of software, classroom and professional blogs, document cameras, LCD projectors, a diverse array of powerful calculators, ever more powerful computers, and interactive whiteboards! It is simply impossible to do the job without collaboration!

Quality

Too often, for a range of legitimate and not so legitimate reasons, we punt, we settle for, we cut corners, we don't polish stones, and we fail to reflect and revise. Again, we're not bad or incompetent and we work hard, but quality and improvement are not as high on the agenda as they might be. Alternatively, consider shared models of excellence. You see a strong vision of teaching and learning, a library of well-developed and validated lesson plans, annotated videos of quality instruction, and exemplars of student work.

Accountability

Too often we face a litany of the "yeah, buts." It's the kids. They don't do their homework. They don't know their facts. They just don't care. It's their parents. It's the elementary program and teachers who don't know math. It's the middle school and those teachers who don't know any math. Alternatively, consider a set of mind-sets that contain ideas like

- I can meet them three-quarters of the way.
- I can strive to engage them with interesting tasks.
- I can take affirmative actions to reteach rather than blame.
- I can hold myself accountable for their learning so long as they try just a little.

In other words: Until and unless we are treated—and we treat each other—with dignity and respect, there will not be enough trust for transparency. Until and unless we have much greater transparency and openness (a mind-set that we can learn from each other), there are few incentives to collaborate. Until and unless we collaborate and remember that learning (our students' as well as our own) is a socially mediated process, it is unlikely we will significantly improve the overall quality of our work. And until and unless this foundation is built, there is insufficient support and an inadequate culture for meaningful accountability that ensures that every student who tries has the opportunity to learn.

7

Changing the System
Assuring Quality of Program Components[*]

Too often it appears that policy makers believe that changes like those advocated in this book can be mandated from above or implemented by fiat of some sort. Nothing is further from the truth or more likely to result in demoralization, frustration, and little real change. Researchers of school change and those who have successfully made improvements understand that teaching resides within a system and that changing teaching requires changes in the system. Frequently lost in the discussions about new standards for curriculum and about shifting instructional practices is the need for a set of *program delivery standards* that support curricular and instructional changes.

While working to implement systemic change within schools, math departments, and school districts, the following fifteen program componets have emerged as a set of critical elements that support a high-performance mathematics program. Considered individually, these fifteen components represent a program checklist of the key separate components. Considered as a whole, these fifteen components represent the complete system of elements that constitutes a program. While a strong program can certainly be implemented in the absence of one or more of these standards, attending to all of them significantly increases the chances that the transition to sensible, sense-making mathematics will be positive and productive. That is why each deserves careful thought and consideration by all principals and other school leaders, particularly as schools and districts move toward implementation of the Common Core State Standards for Mathematics. These fifteen components are:

1. Curriculum

2. Instructional Materials

3. Instructional Technology

---

[*] Chapter 7 is an adaption of Chapter 3 of *A Guide to K–12 Program Development in Mathematics*, copyright 1999 by the Connecticut State Board of Education. Adapted with permission.

4. Instructional Time

5. Instructional Connections

6. Assessment of Students

7. Professional Interaction

8. Professional Development

9. Professional Supervision and Evaluation

10. Monitoring Programs

11. Tracking and Leveling

12. Intervention and Student Support

13. Articulation and Alignment

14. Resource Personnel and Leadership

15. Administrative Understanding and Support

This chapter presents each of these fifteen components with a statement of the standard and a brief elaboration that describes the key elements of a program that meets the standard. Any and all discussions and planning relating to the improvement of mathematics programs must attend to each of these components.

CURRICULUM

A high-quality mathematics program is defined, guided, and supported by a comprehensive, developmentally appropriate, written curriculum that is consistent with the vision of the NCTM Standards and the Common Core State Standards for Mathematics and includes examples and unit/chapter pacing guidance.

Too often, a district's curriculum guide gathers dust in a bottom drawer. Too often, summer curriculum committee work merely codifies the table of contents of the adopted textbook. And too often, teachers are given a series of conflicting messages to "follow the text," "follow the curriculum guide," and "get students ready for the test." These problems can be overcome when a mathematics program is driven by a comprehensive, teacher-friendly curriculum guide that provides clear direction, articulation between grades and courses, and coherence among the program's components. In the era of Common Core State Standards, a district's mathematics curriculum should begin, for each grade or course, with the content and practice standards delineated in the Common Core.

A school or district's mathematics curriculum should also delineate the overarching philosophy and goals of the program; present the key objectives or outcomes for each grade level or course; provide illustrative examples, tasks, and/or activities; indicate how the outcomes or objectives will be assessed; include guidance for pacing units or chapters; and list available resources for implementing the curriculum. In addition, the K–12 curriculum should assure smooth transition from grade to grade and course to course. In short, written curriculum guides should provide clear answers to teachers and others to the questions: What exactly are my students expected to learn this year? and What skills, concepts, and understandings should I be held accountable for teaching this year?

INSTRUCTIONAL MATERIALS

A high-quality mathematics program provides each student with, and makes effective use of, appropriate instructional print materials, as well as provides an adequate supply of nonprint materials to accomplish the goals of the curriculum.

Mathematics used to be the easiest of all major disciplines to support financially. Purchase one textbook for each student and an accompanying teacher's guide for each teacher, place some blank paper, lined paper, and graph paper in each classroom, ensure that each teacher has a blackboard and an ample supply of chalk, and maybe provide an overhead projector. While these limited materials may have worked well to deliver a program limited to the mastery of arithmetic, they are insufficient to support a high-quality mathematics curriculum.

In addition to a core text or, increasingly, a set of core modules, complete with print and online components, teachers need ready access to alternative textbooks, supplemental print materials, measuring devices, geometric models, and a host of grade-level or course-appropriate manipulative materials. Increasingly, teachers need a web-connected computer and either a projector or interactive whiteboard to make efficient use of a broad range of applets and other web-based resources that support teaching and learning. In addition, teachers need access to a projection device (e.g., overhead projector or document camera) to help present material visually and copying machines to quickly and efficiently reproduce diverse instructional materials and assessments that support the instructional program.

Without access to such an array of nontext materials, teachers' ability to deliver the kind of active instruction envisioned in this book is severely compromised.

INSTRUCTIONAL TECHNOLOGY

A high-quality mathematics program ensures that each student has access to necessary technological tools and makes full use of calculators and computer software to implement the goals of the curriculum.

In every sector of our society, technology has changed how we do business, how we manufacture things, how we stay informed, and how we live our lives. Sadly, most schools still lag far behind other institutions when it comes to making full use of technology as a tool to provide greater access to mathematical ideas. The time has come for schools to enter the technological era and shift the fundamental delivery system of education in ways not seen since the invention of books and movable type in the fifteenth century.

Technology, particularly calculators that are now as commonplace as pencils, web-based applets and instructional resources that graphically and interactively help bring mathematical ideas to life, interactive probes that make algebra come alive, spreadsheets and graphing utilities that permeate the business world, online tutors and instructional videos, and word-processing capability, must be available and incorporated into the K–12 mathematics program. Just as it is inconceivable to run a bank with the ledger cards of old or a supermarket with the manual cash registers of yesterday, it is impossible to build a high-quality mathematics program with use of just paper and pencil.

Document cameras and interactive whiteboards enable enhanced displays of student work and more effective time on task. Interactive software enables instruction with powerful dynamic representations. Technology in the form of clickers enables instantaneous, nonjudgmental feedback.

In addition, every teacher of mathematics must recognize that technology has made some mathematics entirely obsolete (e.g., calculating cube roots), some mathematics newly accessible to students (e.g., exponential functions), and some mathematics possible for the first time (e.g., fractals). For this reason, an effective K–12 mathematics program is built on the following assumptions:

- All students have access to appropriate calculators beginning no later than grade 4.
- All teachers have a web-connected classroom demonstration computer with an appropriate projection device.
- All classrooms have a document camera, also connected to a projection device.
- All schools have site-licensed tool and utility software readily available for students' and teachers' use to enhance student learning of mathematics.

INSTRUCTIONAL TIME

A high-quality mathematics program provides scheduled time for mathematics instruction of at least one hour per day for formal mathematics instruction, supplemented less formally through interdisciplinary activities and homework.

It is self-evident that time—formal allocations of minutes per day, informal and interdisciplinary minutes per week, and the overall quality of how the time is used—is a critical variable in assuring a high-quality program. Students whose formal mathematics period is sixty minutes per day receive nearly 180 hours of instruction a year, fully 50 percent more time than students in forty-minute periods. Moreover, students who complete twenty minutes of meaningful homework four nights per week spend over forty additional hours per school year engaged in mathematical tasks. Similarly, students in classes where the daily routine involves significant class time going over homework and starting on new homework receive far less productive instructional time than those in classes where students are actively involved in exploring, investigating, and solving problems.

Thus, the sixty-minute-per-day recommendation represents *a necessary minimum* guideline intended to ensure that schools schedule enough time for teachers and students to be reasonably able to meet the goals of the curriculum. Time allocations of forty-five minutes per day at the elementary level or forty-seven-minute daily class periods at the secondary level may have been acceptable when the primary goal of mathematics was *procedural* fluency for *some* students. It should be clear that meeting the goals of *procedural, conceptual, and problem-solving* fluency by *all* students requires more time as well as more efficient use of that time. When teachers are appropriately expected to conduct meaningful daily warm-ups, actively engage students in *doing* mathematically appropriate activity, conduct summaries and debriefs of this activity, and close with appropriate formative assessment of the lesson goals, it should be clear that allocating less than one hour per day seriously compromises any chance of providing this level of instruction.

It should also be understood that the mathematics program must be connected to the mathematics that is embedded in the science, social studies, and vocational education curricula. It is also expected that these time allocations are supplemented through interdisciplinary and integrated tasks and units and by the ongoing, everyday use of mathematics to solve school and classroom problems. In addition, nothing in this standard should preclude the scheduling of longer blocks of time to allow students to become more deeply involved in activities and projects, or ensuring that students requiring additional support or intervention (see Standard 12) receive significantly more time for learning mathematics.

Many middle and high schools have effectively employed a block schedule that provides for longer class periods, fewer classes per day for both students and teachers, and fewer students per teacher per semester.

INSTRUCTIONAL CONNECTIONS

A high-quality mathematics program regularly makes connections both within mathematics and between mathematics and other subject areas so that students make and see the connections among the major mathematics curriculum strands and between mathematics and other disciplines.

For too long, for too many students, learning mathematics has meant moving from topic to topic, and from chapter to chapter, with little regard to the connections between and among these topics or chapters and even less attention to the connections between the topics and their application in the world and in other disciplines. This lack of connection results in students being forced to learn and memorize far too many bits of information without the benefit of generalizing principles or real-world contexts that make learning easier, more enjoyable, and more significant. A stronger focus on problem solving and greater attention to interdisciplinary approaches tend to naturally support these instructional connections.

One of the hallmarks, first, of the NCTM Standards, and now, of the Common Core State Standards is the emphasis on mathematical connections as a critical feature of mathematics instruction. Rather than continue to view the mathematics curriculum as composed of several discrete strands—computation, measurement, geometry, data, algebra—that are often taught in isolation, a high-quality program regularly fosters connections between and among these strands as well as links the mathematics to everyday experiences and other disciplines.

ASSESSMENT OF STUDENTS

A high-quality mathematics program has a coherent system of common unit or chapter assessments and common grade-level or course summative assessments that are closely aligned with the curricular and instructional goals of the program and that promote the ongoing improvement of instruction.

At the school, department, and classroom levels, the most powerful and informative assessments are the common unit or chapter assessments created or adapted by teachers to assess the degree to which the specific content of a unit or chapter has been mastered. Such common benchmark or interim assessments, situated closest to the curriculum and the teacher, serve as the glue that drives collective attention to what should be taught and how well it is learned. Similarly, a system of common end-of-grade and end-of-course summative assessments provides critical data about the degree to which students have learned what is expected and what parts of the curriculum have not been adequately mastered. Unfortunately, too many schools and districts leave this key piece of the program up to the whims and preferences of individual teachers and thereby fail to build common measures of higher quality and closer alignment with expectations.

In corporate America it is said that "what is inspected, is respected." Similarly, in schools, what is assessed and how it is assessed communicate most clearly what is valued. If the vision of a curriculum oriented to thinking, reasoning, and problem solving is to become a reality, our entire system of assessment and how we hold students accountable must shift. The traditional right/wrong forms of assessment may have been appropriate for assessing the success of a rule-driven, fact-oriented curriculum, but it is increasingly clear that such forms of testing are insufficient to support the curricular and instructional changes that are needed. In fact, our entire system of accountability must shift from the relative standards of percentages above, at, and below advanced, proficient, and basic, to more absolute standards of quality and more holistic judgments of student work, based on clear criteria for expected performance that hold students accountable for meeting high standards. The need to make these more sophisticated judgments is one of the reasons for significant increases in various types of performance assessment being advocated as measures of student achievement and the prominent role such tasks are expected to play in the new generation of high-stakes mathematics assessment.

Accordingly, a high-quality mathematics program must incorporate more powerful assessments of demonstrated accomplishment, using performances, rich tasks, and projects that capture the Common Core standards of mathematics practice in ways that are impossible with multiple-choice items.

When one defines assessment as a process of gathering evidence about a student's knowledge of, ability to use, and disposition toward mathematics and of making inferences from that evidence for a variety of purposes, one begins to see assessment as the third interdependent component of a triangle: curriculum (what to teach), instruction (how to teach), and assessment (how well has learning occurred).

PROFESSIONAL INTERACTION

A high-quality mathematics program ensures that teachers have ample time, formal and informal opportunities, and diverse mechanisms to interact and grow as members of professional learning communities that focus on substantive matters of curriculum, instruction, and assessment.

It is no secret that the typical teacher spends most of his or her time professionally isolated from colleagues. Too rarely do teachers observe each other teaching or study videos of each other at work in the classroom. Too often, professional interaction focuses on scheduling, assignments, or textbook adoptions, not on curricular problems or instructional practices.

The magnitude of the change that teachers of mathematics are being asked to make requires far greater opportunities for substantive professional interaction. This interaction can and must take many forms. For example, peer observations, team-teaching, formal and informal opportunities for sharing, videoing instruction, issue-focused faculty meeting discussions, cross-district grade-level meetings, action research teams, course committees, and common planning time are all powerful vehicles for reducing professional isolation and enhancing professional interaction. Each of these strategies has a role so that school faculties and mathematics departments can become dynamic communities of learners rather than just assortments of teachers and students working in the same building or district. And each of these strategies promotes the sharing of ideas, experiences, and knowledge that is the hallmark of professional collaboration.

The professional interaction described in this standard envisions teachers as collaborative leaders, not as passive followers. It envisions teachers forming study groups, conducting informal research in their classes, and engaging in the inquiry that embodies lifelong learning.

PROFESSIONAL DEVELOPMENT

A high-quality mathematics program is supported by a comprehensive program of professional development that focuses on issues of curriculum, instruction, and assessment; recognizes the importance of ongoing professional growth, and provides opportunities to participate in conferences, seminars, and institutes.

Once again, in light of the magnitude of the change that teachers of mathematics are being asked to make, it must be broadly and clearly understood that it is entirely unreasonable to expect teachers of mathematics to implement these changes in curriculum, instruction, and assessment when they are unaware of available programs, resources, and materials, and when there is so little time for reflection on these changes. Without planned, sustained, and ongoing professional development, including opportunities to attend conferences and seminars, access to professional journals, encouragement to visit with colleagues, and time for reflection, teachers too often remain unaware of the paths to change and improvement. In fact, many observers of Japanese schools cite the time allocated to precisely these forms of professional development and professional interaction as one of the starkest differences between the two systems.

For these reasons, an ongoing system of professional development for teachers of mathematics that is responsive to identified instructional needs, adequately funded, and supported with sufficient time must be in place within every school and district. In addition to the professional interaction strategies described above, professional development opportunities scheduled for after school, weekends, and summer must be supplemented with released-time opportunities within the school day that allow for such powerful approaches as co-teaching opportunities, collaborative planning sessions, lesson study, instructional rounds, gallery teaching, and video analysis.

PROFESSIONAL SUPERVISION AND EVALUATION

A high-quality mathematics program includes a system of professional supervision and evaluation that sets high standards of professional performance and is supported by programs and policies to assure both that these standards are met and that teachers have sufficient support to meet them.

Just as the methods and techniques of student assessment must change to account for measuring newer and broader outcomes, so too must methods and techniques of teacher evaluation change to account for different definitions of productivity and effectiveness.

The commonplace practice of casual and infrequent classroom observation, often carried out in a perfunctory manner, insufficiently drives the improvement in practice and, thus, student achievement. Indeed, professional evaluation that supports a high-quality mathematics program needs to be broadened in scope and deepened in rigor. Administrators, supervisors, and coaches must be better trained and must be more knowledgeable about effective mathematics curriculum and instruction. In addition, professional evaluation must go beyond periodic observations and include such activities as the development and peer review of professional performance portfolios, analysis of student work and student achievement, and the periodic use of assessment center activities like those used by the National Board for Professional Teaching Standards.

It is critical that classroom teachers receive constructive support—as they are supervised *and* as they are evaluated—so that excellence in teaching becomes a realistic and attainable goal for all. This means that the entire process of coaching, supervision, and evaluation entails feedback and clear prescriptions for action. Observations conducted without follow-up are unprofessional and do not foster change. Conversely, observations of classroom practice, analysis of student work and student achievement scores that are carried out in a collegial spirit of discussion, feedback, and planning are far more professional and far more likely to result in improvement.

MONITORING PROGRAMS

A high-quality mathematics program has a set of coordinated procedures that provide ongoing monitoring and periodic evaluation of the entire program to assure that student achievement goals are being met.

Every program in every school system should be periodically subjected to careful scrutiny. Those within the system—and increasingly, those outside the system—have a right to definitive answers to questions such as the following:

- Is the program working for all students? If not, why not and what can be done to change this situation?
- Is the curriculum meeting the needs of students and the broader society? If not, why not and what can be done to change this situation?
- Is instruction provided in ways that maximize student achievement? If not, why not and what can be done to change this situation?
- Are students achieving in sufficient numbers and at high enough levels? If not, why not and what can be done to change this situation?
- Are all necessary program components in place and aligned to achieve program goals? If not, why not and what can be done to change this situation?

Additionally, for every grade or course or program component, effective programs gather data and implement plans that address the following questions:

- What are we doing well and how do we know?
- How can we expand or extend what is working well?
- What is not going well or in need of attention and how do we know?
- Why has this issue not been addressed?
- What can we do to improve what is not working well or in need of attention?

To ensure a high-quality mathematics program, it is necessary to conduct periodic and comprehensive reviews of the entire program, as well as specific grades and courses, to answer these and other questions, publicly report findings, and implement changes on the basis of the review.

TRACKING AND LEVELING

A high-quality mathematics program minimizes the leveling, sorting, and tracking of students while fully meeting the diverse and individual needs of all students.

No single component of the educational system more powerfully communicates the expectations—both high and low—we hold for young people than the ways in which schools sort, level, and track students. A major step in moving toward the vision of "mathematics for *all*" is a dramatic decrease in the ability-grouping, leveling, and tracking of students. This does not mean abandoning all ability groups, it does not mean the elimination of all honors courses, and it does not mean all students grouped heterogeneously all the time. It does mean, however, a change in policy at the school and district levels regarding ability-grouping and tracking so that no student is denied access to a rich and demanding mathematics program best suited to his or her individual needs and interests. In addition, such a policy recognizes that flexible grouping and collaborative teaching *can* be appropriate strategies for best meeting individual needs and helping to support inclusion practices.

Stated differently, it must be recognized that the current gap in breadth, depth, and rigor between what is provided for the top 20 percent and for the bottom 20 percent must be narrowed significantly by raising expectations for the bottom 20 percent. However, it must also be recognized that it is *not* reasonable that expectations for the top 10 percent be identical to those for the bottom 10 percent.

INTERVENTION AND STUDENT SUPPORT

A high-quality mathematics program provides supplemental instructional services to assure that all students have the opportunity to meet the goals and expectations of the program.

While individual and diverse backgrounds, interests, learning styles or preferences, and abilities are widely recognized, schools often overlook, and even ignore, these differences by keeping learning *time* a constant. There are one-year courses, forty-five-minute classes, fifteen-minute quizzes, and two-minute fact drills that apply to all students. Common sense dictates that while some students need less time, others need more time to be able to reasonably meet the goals for any lesson, unit, year, or program. One way that time becomes a variable used to better meet individual student needs is through the provision of extra, remedial, or compensatory instruction for those students for whom traditional time allocations are insufficient.

For example, the three levels of Response to Intervention suggest that the first line of attack (Level 1) is high-quality, differentiated instruction in all mainstream classrooms where the diverse mathematical needs of approximately 85 percent of students can be met. The second line of attack (Level 2) is supplemental programming in addition to the mainstream program for about approximately 10 percent of students, wherein they have additional time during the school day for extra or extended opportunities to learn, ideally using instructional approaches that match students' learning needs and styles. Finally, at Level 3, for those 5 percent to 7 percent of students for whom the mainstream classroom is unlikely to meet their needs, high-quality special education in self-contained or resource rooms is available.

In addition to time adjustments, effective remedial and supplemental interventions must also address adjustments in instructional methods and formats. For example, among the conditions that support more effective student learning are:

- teachers who possess a wide repertoire of strategies—including a focus on alternative approaches to doing mathematics and multiple representations of mathematical ideas as well as assorted instructional materials, including hands-on materials and high-quality software—and who supplement daily instruction for needy students;

- math centers that are well stocked with materials, supplemental print and electronic resources, and computers, and that are staffed with trained and knowledgeable personnel;

- after-hours programs such as after-school tutoring clinics, Saturday academies, and summer enrichment programs; and

- support personnel available to work with students within classrooms rather than in pull-out situations and who work closely with regular classroom teachers.

ARTICULATION AND ALIGNMENT

A high-quality mathematics program evolves coherently, grade by grade and course by course, from kindergarten to twelfth grade and displays an alignment of curriculum, instructional materials, professional development, and assessment that are all implemented to attain the overarching goals of the program.

Two often-noted characteristics of what has been referred to as the "underachieving mathematics curriculum" are the mixed, and often conflicting, messages given to teachers about what should be taught, how it should be taught, and how it will be assessed on the one hand, and the lack of a smooth flow of mathematical content as students progress from kindergarten to twelfth grade on the other hand. Among the potential benefits of the Common Core State Standards for Mathematics is a more coherent program built from cross-grade domains to single-grade clusters of connected standards to focused grade-level standards within cluster. Another promise of the Common Core State Standards is a long overdue system of much greater alignment among the standards, the instructional materials, and the assessments.

While alignment at the macro level around the Common Core is an important step forward, school and district leaders need to minimize the mixed messages that emerge from misalignments at the micro level. This requires that curriculum guides replace textbooks and tests as the primary driver of the program. In addition to delineating content expectations, these curriculum guides need to provide both instructional suggestions and assessment possibilities to ensure tighter alignment. Similarly, curriculum guides must be designed to ensure a developmentally appropriate sequence of outcomes, recognizing the need for exploratory exposure to mathematical ideas, opportunities to work with and master these ideas, and time to review and reinforce these ideas.

A common vehicle for increasing the articulation and coordination of the curriculum is through grade-level meetings of two consecutive grades and meetings of course committees where teachers share problems and concerns and make necessary adjustments.

RESOURCE PERSONNEL AND LEADERSHIP

A high-quality mathematics program assigns the responsibility for the ongoing implementation and improvement of the program to qualified coaches, coordinators, supervisors, resource personnel, and/or department chairs in order to provide support, coordination, supervision, and leadership.

Each of the above components makes it increasingly clear that a high-quality K–12 mathematics program entails a complex web of ongoing activity, evaluation, and support. Such a program cannot just be mandated or in place and be expected to run by itself for some period of time. In fact, like every other aspect of a school system, the effectiveness and vitality of a district's K–12 mathematics program depends critically on the assignment of responsibility for program oversight and coordination to one or more individuals. All too often when program leadership and responsibility for ongoing implementation and improvement are not vested in one or more individuals, the focus on program quality and improvement tends to fall through the cracks and fragment under the weight of other priorities.

Thus, given that high-quality programs require that a vision of reform be created and nurtured, that teachers be kept abreast of changes and aware of professional development opportunities, and that curricular, instructional, and assessment improvement are ongoing processes, it is imperative that leadership of and responsibility for the mathematics program be clearly assigned and maintained at all levels.

ADMINISTRATIVE UNDERSTANDING AND SUPPORT

A high-quality mathematics program receives strong support from principals and central office administrators to ensure that these standards are met.

These program delivery standards do not get implemented automatically or because they are listed and described in a curriculum guide. Rather, their implementation requires the understanding and tangible support of principals, curriculum coordinators, assistant superintendents, and superintendents. While implementation of a curriculum and effective delivery of instruction occur in thousands of classrooms, the critical support for teachers and understanding of the program described in this chapter derive from the beliefs and actions of hundreds of school and district administrators.

These administrators are key for setting a tone for continuous review and improvement, for maintaining continually higher expectations, and for providing teachers with the financial, material, and professional development support they need to meet the school or district's objectives. Effective administrators strengthen a mathematics program by encouraging experimentation, by facilitating the review and use of school and district assessment data, and by keeping concern for student achievement in mathematics on the front burner at all times. Effective administrators also "grant permission" for teachers to take risks and shift both curriculum and instruction. Finally, administrators play a key role in encouraging and supporting teachers who are struggling to change old habits and adopt new practices.

Figure 7–1 shows a simple data gathering and planning form for helping any school leader assess the quality of these fifteen components and identify areas that need additional attention.

Figure 7–1   *Assessing the quality of the components of our mathematics program: How are we doing and what must we focus on?*

COMPONENT	OUR STRENGTHS IN THIS COMPONENT	OUR WEAKNESSES IN THIS COMPONENT	ACTIONS TO STRENGTHEN THIS COMPONENT
Curriculum			
Instructional Materials			
Instructional Technology			
Instructional Time			
Instructional Connections			
Assessment of Students			
Professional Interaction			
Professional Development			
Professional Supervision and Evaluation			
Monitoring Programs			
Tracking and Leveling			
Intervention and Student Support			
Articulation and Alignment			
Resource Personnel and Leadership			
Administrative Understanding and Support			

Conclusion
Critical Lessons Learned Along the Way

For the past thirty or so years, I have been blessed. As a mathematics consultant in the Connecticut Department of Education from 1979 to 2001, I had the opportunity to work in dozens of school districts, hundreds of schools, and with thousands of dedicated and professional teachers of mathematics. I had the opportunity to work in an incredibly supportive and collegial State Department of Education where the question "How can we help?" has never been empty rhetoric. Since 2002, I have served as a principal research analyst at the American Institutes for Research in Washington, DC, where I have been able to work with the Microsoft Math Partnership in eight Puget Sound school districts, the General Electric Foundation's Ensuring Futures program in six urban districts, and most recently in several School Improvement Grant "turn-around" schools. I have also had a wealth of varied experiences across the country as part of my activities within the National Council of Teachers of Mathematics and the National Council of Supervisors of Mathematics. Over this period of time and in these various roles, I have seen people make extraordinary changes. I have seen schools undergo major transformations and districts provide truly excellent mathematics programs. But far more often I have watched as ignorance, confusion, fear, a lack of leadership, or simply an unwillingness to move has relegated children and young adults to a truly mind-numbing mathematics program. Through it all—some truly amazing, some good, some bad, and some downright ugly—here is some of what I've learned and what I'd like to pass along to all who toil in the honorable vineyards of making mathematics truly work for all.

First, never stray from *a dogged focus on classroom instruction*. Just as Bill Clinton won in 1992 in part by making "It's the economy, stupid!" a campaign mantra, for educators and educational policy makers at all levels, the appropriate mantra must be "It's the classroom, stupid!" When all is said and done, it's not the buses, the buildings, or the budgets that determine how much and how well students learn, it's the daily interactions between teachers and students, and among students, in the classrooms of every school that determines how much and how well students will learn. New materials, professional development, and effective supervision are all important only to the degree they support high-quality instructional interactions. When things are going well and students are learning, the causal path leads directly back to the classroom. Similarly, when things are not going well, when results are mediocre at best, and when students are bored and acting out, the same causal path points to the classroom. If one seeks to improve the quality of education and the quantity of student achievement, enhancing, empowering, energizing, and engaging teaching and teachers has always been and will continue to be the optimal choice.

Second, I have come to believe that *assessment is the most powerful change lever in our arsenal.* Good tests nudge along improvements and push people to make change. Bad tests perpetuate mediocrity and reinforce counterproductive practices. In the daily lives of most teachers and students it is the high-stakes assessments that are used that communicate what we value. Think how often students ask "Is this going to be on the test?" When told "Yes," pencils and notebooks start to stir and attention gets paid. When told "No, this is just enrichment," eyes start to glaze over and heads start to nod. That's why improving and better aligning high-stakes state assessments has been one of the most popular strategies for encouraging change. And that's why building influential and respected grade-level criterion-referenced tests and common course final examinations are often more important than the curriculum upon which they are purportedly based. Anyone interested in what is valued in the intended curriculum need look no further than the tests that students are given. When these tests regularly include interesting problems, extended tasks, explanations of reasoning, and justifications for actions and solutions, one can be sure reform is being supported and encouraged and that the learning of important mathematics is being stressed.

Third, as I have tried to exemplify throughout this book, *everything we advocate must be grounded in concrete examples.* All good instruction is enhanced by examples that help the learner build on prior experiences, connect new ideas, concretize new concepts, and apply what is being learned. The same must be true in all our discussions about shifting mathematics programs. Unfortunately, as educators, we too often fall back upon the words of lectures and the abstractions of concepts, forgetting to consistently link our words and abstractions to what can actually be illustrated. That's why we must pause and show each other exactly what we mean with clear and compelling examples. And that's why exemplars, models, samples of student work, and videos are indispensable tools for helping people to understand our ideas and our vision.

Fourth, we need to *toot our own horns* much more frequently and much more loudly that we are often comfortable doing. There is so much that is good in America's elementary, middle, and high schools. There is much mathematics learning that is working well for millions of students. And there are thousands of pockets of extraordinary accomplishments that occur daily in America's classrooms. But one would hardly know these things in the face of an incessant onslaught of news about the problems, the woes, and the failures of our schools. In far too many cases, we educators are our own worst enemies: At best, we think it's unprofessional and unbecoming to taut our successes, and at worst, we express our frustrations in public and reinforce the ever-present negative perceptions. An important part of the best solution is to become our own public relations officers. At all levels of the system, it is time to gather data on what is working, celebrate successes with great fanfare, and publicize our not inconsiderable accomplishments. All corporations have public information personnel who are assigned to churn out the good news and put the best possible spin on events. Every politician either has a press secretary or acts as his or her own press agent to inform, promote, and publicize. Every school and every district should engage in commensurate promotion of the positive.

Finally, each of us must remember *how much difference one person can make*. The enduring, yet haunting, beauty of the education profession is that each and every educator has the potential to make an extraordinary difference in the lives of students. But it is usually years before that difference is recognized, and rarely then is it even acknowledged. More often recognized, but no more frequently acknowledged, is the extraordinary difference every educator can make in the lives of colleagues. Thus, in classrooms and faculty rooms, in school, district, and state agency offices, the motivating force that makes educators so special is the understanding that taking the extra minute, going the extra mile, reaching out one additional time can, and often does, make the critical difference. Recognizing and acting on this simple truth can, and does, allow each of us to touch eternity.

Appendices

IT'S TIME TO ABANDON COMPUTATIONAL DRUDGERY
(But Not the Computation)

It's time to recognize that, for many students, real mathematical power, on the one hand, and facility with long pencil-and-paper computational procedures, on the other, are mutually exclusive. In fact, it's time to acknowledge that continuing to teach these increasingly obsolete skills to our students is not only unnecessary but counterproductive and downright dangerous!

My intent in so brashly taking on one of the lingering pillars of basic elementary education is neither to be unduly confrontational nor impishly irresponsible. I am not seeking to wrap myself in the banner of radical reformers or to stir up the fundamentalists. Rather, my purpose is to raise an issue that is not going to disappear. It's an issue that must be discussed openly and honestly, and then resolved swiftly and clearly if we are to realize our aspirations for truly world-class schools.

First let's clarify exactly what is being proposed. This is *not* about reducing emphasis on one-digit addition, subtraction, multiplication, and division facts. These facts and the self-confidence that comes with their mastery are more important than ever. Nor is this about abandoning computation, which remains an indispensable part of the mathematics program, so long as it is done mentally, with a calculator, or via estimation. It *is* about the formal paper-and-pencil computational procedures that constitute the core grade-school mathematical experiences of most American youngsters. It's about mindless procedures like "carrying threes into the tens column," "six times seven is forty-two, put down two and carry the four," and "eight from two, can't do, cross out the five, make it a four, and borrow ten." It's also about memorized rules like "Yours is not to reason why, just invert and multiply" that, for most students, meaninglessly enter one ear and leave the other.

Usually this is all it takes to start an avalanche of dismay. The most common reactions are: "But weren't those rules and procedures good enough for us?" "Isn't this just the 'new math' all over again?" "But what if the calculator is lost or the batteries die?" and "What about the basics?" So let's make the case. Let's begin with what we know and what most of us can agree upon. Then let's see how acting on these agreements leads naturally and logically to abandoning computational drudgery.

We know that less than a generation ago, real people in real situations regularly put pencil to paper, used a little understood procedure that had been practiced to the point of automaticity, and computed a solution to a problem involving numbers. Without the rote ability to perform the procedure, the needed solution was usually unattainable. We know with equal clarity that this is no longer how the real world works. All around us, real people in real situations regularly put finger to button and make critical decisions about which buttons to press, not where and how to carry threes into hundreds columns. We understand that this change is on the order of magnitude of the outhouse to indoor plumbing in terms of comfort and convenience, and of the sundial to digital timepieces in terms of accuracy and accessibility.

We also know that a curriculum dominated by a strict hierarchy of skills and proce-dures has meshed perfectly with the historically perceived mission that schools serve as society's primary sorting mechanism. What better vehicle for anointing the few and cast-ing out the many than demanding mastery of increasingly complex computational pro-cedures—most often taught and learned in mindless, rote fashion? And how else can we account for the obeisance paid to the norm-referenced standardized test's bell curve of student achievement? But what is increasingly clear is how radically society's needs and expectations for schools have shifted. No longer are schools expected to serve as social and economic sorting machines. Instead, schools must become empowering machines. No longer simply perpetuators of the bell curve, where only some survive and even fewer truly thrive, schools and their mathematics programs must instill understanding and confidence in all. In short, we now understand that teaching formal rules for adding and subtracting decimals, like their "gone-and-not-missed" cousin, the square root algorithm, remains a vestige of a sort-'em-out approach that continues to fail both kids and the soci-ety that so desperately needs a far more mathematically powerful citizenry.

We also know that we must differentiate the proverbial baby from the bath water. The "baby" is having a $10 bill and seeing that Big Macs are $1.59 each. It's formulating questions about change and taxes, and it's figuring out how many could be bought. The core of mathematical power is explaining why you think six Big Macs is a reasonable estimate and why division is an appropriate operation in this situation. It's interpreting the 6.2893082 on the calculator display, or it's presenting alternative approaches using repetitive addition, repetitive subtraction, or trial and error with the multiplication key. Meanwhile, the "bath water" is a pencil-and-paper procedure for dividing 10 by 1.59 on which no sane person relies. We know that it's time to change the "bath water" lest the "baby" continue to drown.

But none of this is as compelling as what we know about the sense of failure and the pain unnecessarily imposed on hundreds of thousands of students in the name of mastering these obsolete procedures. We know that many students are bored to death and frustrated to tears when faced with completing "exercises #1–29 (odd) on page 253." Compare the energy and enthusiasm of a class cooperatively learning statistics with bags of M&Ms to a class mindlessly and individually inverting and multiplying meaningless fractions to arrive at equally meaningless answers. Compare a class where students are estimating costs for a shopping spree from newspaper fliers prior to using calculators to see who comes closest to $100 to a class tediously finding sums of columns of numbers with no connection to children's lives.

A few short years ago we had few or no alternatives to pencil-and-paper computa-tion. A few short years ago we could even justify the pain and frustration we witnessed in our classes as necessary parts of learning what were then important skills. Today there are alternatives and there is no honest way to justify the psychic toll it takes. We need to admit that computational drill and practice devour an incredibly large proportion of instructional time, precluding any real chance for actually applying mathematics and developing the conceptual understanding that underlies mathematical literacy.

So why do we continue to impose these skills on our students and teachers? Because despite all the powerful reasons for change, schools are equally powerful perpetuators of what they've always done. Ask an educator why long division is still taught and one will hear that it's in the text, on the test, part of the curriculum, and/or has always been taught. Never does one hear that it's needed or that it's important.

If we are true to our professed goals, the course is clear. It's time to build mathematics programs that engage and empower, unencumbered by the discriminatory shackles of computational drudgery. It's time to banish these vestiges of yesteryear from our schools and from our tests.

Adapted from the author's "It's Time to Abandon Computational Algorithms," *Education Week*, February 9, 1994.

MOVING MATHEMATICS OUT OF MEDIOCRITY

The logic for the importance of improving school mathematics programs is reasonably unassailable. The country's long-term economic security and social well-being are clearly linked to sustained innovation and workplace productivity. This innovation and productivity rely, just as clearly, on the quality of human capital and equity of opportunity that, in turn, emerge from high-quality education, particularly in the areas of literacy, mathematics, and science. Applying the if-then deductive logic of classical geometry puts a strong K–12 mathematics program at the heart of America's long-term economic viability.

But the problems with mathematics in the United States are just as clear. A depressingly comprehensive, yet honest, appraisal must conclude that our typical math curriculum is generally incoherent, skill-oriented, and accurately characterized as "a mile wide and an inch deep." It is dispensed via ruthless tracking practices and focused mainly on the "one right way to get the one right answer" approach to solving problems that few normal human beings have any real need to consider. Moreover, it is assessed by fifty-one high-stakes tests of marginal quality and overwhelmingly implemented by undersupported and professionally isolated teachers who too often rely on "show-tell-practice" modes of instruction that ignore powerful research findings about better ways to convey mathematical knowledge.

For twenty years, we have tinkered at the margins, merely adjusting parts of the system while ignoring the fact that the basic structure has remained largely intact and underperforming. During those twenty years, we've raised achievement a little and narrowed gaps a bit. But even as the need for broader and deeper mathematical literacy has grown, our traditional approach still rarely works for more than a third of our students, and it fails even more when it comes to critical-reasoning and problem-solving skills. It shouldn't be all that surprising that on the 2006 Program for International Student Assessment, or PISA, fifteen-year-old U.S. students placed an unacceptable twenty-fifth out of thirty countries tested.

Fortunately, the solutions are as clear as the problems. The answers do not revolve around costly new initiatives. Moving beyond mediocrity does not have to mean new textbooks and supplemental programs, or a slew of new calculators and computers, or jumping on the latest bandwagon of benchmark assessments. Instead, our attention needs to focus on how effectively existing programs are implemented, how available technology is integrated and used to enhance the learning of skills and concepts, and why assessments that steal valuable instructional time must provide relevant information that is actually put to use to inform revisions and reteaching.

In short, it's time to turn to the real basics of what we expect students to learn, how we convey that, how we measure student learning, and how we support teachers and reduce their isolation.

We need first to recognize that most of our major economic competitors, and nearly all of the highest-scoring countries on international assessments, have a national set of mathematics standards that guarantees a degree of coherence, focus, and alignment absent in the patchwork of state standards in the United States. A nationally mandated curriculum isn't the answer. But a broadly accepted, strongly recommended set of world-class national mathematics standards for grades K–12 is. Such standards would provide informed guidance and attract widespread interest, yet would not fall under the antiquated rubric of "local control."

If we took this route, textbooks could be revamped to cut redundancy and add depth and balance between procedural and conceptual understanding. The recommended math standards could delineate sensible and reasonable expectations for students at each grade level and in each course. Curriculum sequences and objectives could be crafted so that all students would reach key elements of algebra in eighth grade and leave high school with sufficient understanding of both calculus and statistics. These skills would help them thrive in the workplace and at postsecondary institutions.

Second, we need to examine what common sense, observation, and research tell us about instructional practices that make significant differences in student achievement. Such practices can be found in high-performing schools across the country. There, we see teachers making "Why?" a classroom mantra to support a culture of reasoning and justification. We see cumulative review being incorporated daily. We see deliberately planned lessons that skillfully employ alternative approaches and multiple representations that value different ways to reach solutions to real problems. We see teachers relying on relevant contexts and using questions to create language-rich mathematics classrooms.

Good mathematics instruction is hard, but it isn't quantum physics, yet few vehicles are currently used to model and institutionalize these techniques that make a difference. That is why compassionate, collegial, and yet candid coaching and supervision, guided by a compelling vision of high-quality mathematics instruction, can make such a tremendous difference in how much students learn and how teaching skills are strengthened.

Third, we need to address the current mishmash of assessments that has emerged from implementation of the federal No Child Left Behind Act. How can one expect instruction to focus on conceptual understanding, or communicating one's thinking, or reasoning through a complex problem, when tests hold students accountable for only low-level skills and multiple-choice answers? Accountability isn't the problem. The problem rests with the instruments being used to hold the system accountable.

We should look at what characterizes student assessments in other countries. Most of Singapore's tests, for example, consist of problem-oriented, constructed-response items. PISA's items are set in realistic contexts and require thinking and reasoning about substantive mathematics, as opposed to recall and regurgitation of tangential content. Moving forward, we must look to the federal government and its research-and-development muscle and investment to create high-quality national assessments of mathematics at the ends of grades 4, 8, and 10. Until this happens, we will continue to muddle through multiple and meaningless standards with mixed signals and continued mediocrity.

Establishing a set of high-stakes, high-quality, annually released national assessments will drive improvement, reduce the current hodgepodge of state assessments, and move the United States toward a rational alignment between what is taught and what is tested.

Finally, we need to address professional isolation among teachers. It is the nature of the profession that most educators practice their craft behind closed doors. They usually go about their work unobserved and undersupported. Far too often, teachers revert to how they were taught, not how their effective colleagues are teaching. Common problems are often solved individually rather than collaboratively.

Successful enterprises don't tolerate such conditions. We must change the professional culture of teaching. Principals must develop innovative ways to facilitate professional sharing and interaction. Middle and high school math departments must become true communities of learners.

In an example of this strategy in motion, teachers in one enterprising district I have visited regularly share and discuss their videotaped lessons. After two years of their doing so, the district finds that marginal teachers have become good teachers, and good teachers have become even better. Simultaneously, classroom practices have become far more transparent, and discussions now focus on specific instructional strategies. Common problems are approached and solved collaboratively.

It is time to recognize math education as a critical component of America's economic infrastructure. National interest supports a military for the country's defense and an interstate highway system for effective commerce. Now, we must support—and demand—a national K–12 mathematics program that far better serves our students, our economy, and our national interest.

Adapted from the author's Commentary, *Education Week*, January 7, 2009.

FOUR TEACHER-FRIENDLY POSTULATES FOR THRIVING IN A SEA OF CHANGE

Many of us went into mathematics teaching because it was always so neat and clean. We felt an affinity toward teaching and learning mathematics because it was orderly and logical. There was almost always only one numerical answer arrived at by using one right procedure that could be easily graded as either right or wrong. We knew that with our beloved mathematics we suffered none of the gray areas that plague the disciplines of language arts and social studies. And we knew that we would be rewarded for teaching mathematics just as we ourselves were taught. But, oh, how things have changed!

Let's face it: The NCTM standards (1989, 1991) have made our professional lives much more challenging. Given how much the teaching of mathematics must change to serve a digitized world of calculators and computers and given the breadth of the recommendations of the standards, it's not surprising that many teachers of mathematics are frustrated and feel thoroughly challenged. To ease this inevitable frustration, I offer four perspective-building postulates for thriving in a sea of change.

Postulate 1: We Are Being Asked to Teach in Distinctly Different Ways from How We Were Taught.

It is a long-accepted truth that most people parent as they were parented and most teachers teach as they were taught. We build on what is familiar because the familiar "feels right." However, to teach concepts, not just skills; to rely on cooperative groups; to work collaboratively with colleagues; and to assume the availability of calculators are all parts of a very unfamiliar terrain for many of us. Neither previous generations of mathematics teachers nor our colleagues in other disciplines have had to face such a chasm between how they were taught and how they are being asked to teach. No wonder many of us are feeling disoriented and inadequate (see Postulate #4).

Since people can't do what people haven't seen or experienced, we need to create tangible and accessible models of curricular and instructional reform. We need to increase opportunities for collegial classroom visits and we need to increase our reliance on videotapes of what the distinctly different forms of pedagogy look like.

Postulate 2: The Traditional Curriculum Was Designed to Meet Societal Needs That No Longer Exist.

The bedrock upon which this entire reform movement rests is a clear understanding that society's needs and expectations for schools have shifted radically. No longer are schools expected to serve as society's primary sorting mechanisms. Instead, schools must become empowering machines. From schools as perpetuators of the bell curve, where only *some* were expected to survive and *even fewer* truly thrive, education must be a springboard where *all* must attain higher levels. This is why behaviors and attitudes that were rewarded a short decade or two ago now are under such scrutiny.

In the face of such emotionally trying bombardments, two very different responses to the standards and other aspects of the reform movement have become common. Some have basically ignored the entire movement, believing that "this too will pass." Others understand that change is required but, sensing that they themselves are not really moving fast enough, begin to feel guilty about not doing more sooner. Denial and guilt are both entirely appropriate responses to the magnitude of the change swirling around us. However, neither response is particularly comforting and neither represents the level of professionalism we expect from ourselves.

For comfort and a professional safety net, I find it helpful to remember that ignoring the need for change in mathematics ignores how radically different society's expectations for schools have become. And feeling guilty about what we've done in the past or about not changing fast enough ignores how effectively schools once met a set of needs that simply no longer exists.

Postulate 3: It Is Unreasonable to Ask a Professional to Change Much More Than 10 Percent a Year, but It is Unprofessional to Change by Much Less Than 10 Percent a Year.

It easily could be argued that the most disorienting element of our lives is the rate at which things are changing. Many have written about people's ability to accommodate to the ever-increasing rate of change. In somewhat arbitrary, but certainly comforting, fashion, I have come to believe that something around 10 percent a year is a reasonable rate to expect. It's large enough to represent real and significant change, but small enough to be manageable.

One way to visualize change at this rate is to think about substituting one new unit into the year or shifting four weeks of instruction to address something new or do something in a very different way, for example, changing questioning techniques or using journals. Using this incremental approach results in a change of nearly half of what we do in five years. Even the most radical proponent of reform should be satisfied with change of this magnitude in our mathematics classes, and even the most cautious and tradition-bound among us should be able to retain a real sense of control over such a rate of change.

Postulate 4: If You Don't Feel Inadequate, You're Probably Not Doing the Job.

Just think what we are asking each other to do: increase the use of technology; use manipulatives and pictures with far greater frequency; make regular use of group work; focus on problems, communication, applications, and interdisciplinary approaches; teach far more heterogeneous groups; increase attention to statistics, geometry, and discrete mathematics; assess students in far more authentic and complex ways; and do it all yesterday and in ways that boost achievement overnight! Feeling overwhelmed by this torrent of change isn't weakness or unprofessional—it's an entirely rational response.

It should be obvious that no one can do it all. Just as no one expects a physician to be an expert in all aspects of medicine, it is just as unreasonable to expect a mathematics teacher in the 1990s to be an expert in all aspects of teaching mathematics. We must select a few areas of focus and balance the fears and worries we understandably have in some areas with the pride of accomplishment and success we find in other areas. We must accept the inevitability of a sense of inadequacy and use it to stimulate the ongoing growth and learning that characterizes the true professional. Only then will we be sufficiently armed, intellectually and emotionally, to thrive in the exhilarating, exhausting, and often overwhelming sea of change.

REFERENCES

Leinwand, Steven J. "Sharing, Supporting, Risk Taking: First Steps to Instructional Reform." *Mathematics Teacher* 85 (September 1992): 466–70.

National Council of Teachers of Mathematics. *Curriculum and Evaluation Standards for School Mathematics*. Reston, VA: The Council, 1989.

———. *Professional Standards for Teaching Mathematics*. Reston, VA: The Council, 1991.

This article first appeared in the *Mathematics Teacher*, September 1994, NCTM and was reprinted in the *Mathematics Teacher*, May 2007.

WHAT THE WORLD NEEDS NOW: MATH TLCs

A plea for refocusing corporate and foundation investment in education to support cadres of Math Teacher Leader Coaches

It's all about the quality of instruction. Despite all the distractions and sincere yet often misguided efforts, when it comes to significantly raising student achievement, the heart of the matter continues to be the *quality of daily classroom instruction* and the degree to which students are provided with *meaningful and effective opportunities to learn.* In mathematics classrooms, research, observations of teaching, and the wisdom of practice are clear about those instructional practices that make significant differences. Effective teachers incorporate daily, cumulative review of skills and concepts into instruction to ensure readiness for new work. Effective teachers make the question "Why?" a classroom mantra to support a culture of reasoning and justification. Effective teachers rely on relevant contexts to engage their students' interest and use questions to stimulate thinking and to create language-rich mathematics classrooms. Lessons are deliberately planned and skillfully employ alternative approaches and multiple representations—including pictures and concrete materials—as part of explanations and answers. Increasingly, it is clear that practices such as these are developed and institutionalized in schools with *effective coaching* supported by teacher leaders and coaches.

Visit some of the most effective schools in any district or state, and you'll find formal or informal coaching. Experienced teachers mentor new teachers. It is not uncommon for colleagues to observe colleagues teaching and then debrief these observations. There are frequent discussions about what worked, what did not work, and what adjustments might be made. Coaches co-plan and co-teach with, and critique the work of, colleagues. Teacher leaders orchestrate collaborative reviews of videotaped lessons and lead seminars around common readings. The debilitating professional isolation of most teachers does not exist. Instead, there is a common spirit of "We're all in this together," a respectful ethos of transparency, and a *culture of professional sharing* orchestrated by teacher leaders and coaches.

Some of my recent observations in one K–8 school follow:

> The third graders were counting by 10s beginning with 570. When they got to 600, their teacher asked "What changed?" and "Why?" to focus attention on the big idea of place value and how 10 more than nine 10s takes us to ten 10s or the next hundred. When students announced that the next number was 610, their teacher asked, "Why 610 and not 601?" to help differentiate the tens place from the ones place and to highlight a common error. What a difference in student learning between this class where these questions were asked and one where they were not asked.

Down the hall, a fifth-grade class was finding the product of 935 and 7. Chris explained her work, displayed from the document camera, as seven 5s make 35, seven 30s make 210 because it's ten times 7×3, and seven 900s make 6,300 because it's one hundred times 7×9. Then $35 + 210 + 6,700$ is 6,945. Next Dana arose and also used the document camera to display and explain the traditional "7 times 5 is 35 so put down the 5 and carry the 3; then 7 times 3 is 21 plus 3 is 24 so put down the 4 and carry the 2 . . . and so the answer is 6,945. Not missing a beat, the teacher asked the class where Chris' 35 shows up in Dana's work and where Dana's 24 appears in Chris' work, thereby engaging the class in a powerful discussion of how the two approaches are related and why both approaches work and how place value and the distributive property underlie both the traditional and the partial product algorithms for multiplication.

And over in seventh grade, when struggling with $5 + (-9)$, some students explained how they "had to move 9 units to the left from positive 5, so 5 units takes them to 0 and since $9 - 5 = 4$, they need to go 4 more units to -4." Other students visualized 5 blue and 9 red chips, created 5 blue-red "zero pairs" and saw that there had to be 4 blue left, giving them an answer of -4. In both cases students were certain of their answer, had confidence in their understanding, and had no trouble explaining their reasoning. Not surprisingly, and fortunately, not one student mimicked what was in the textbook and announced that "since you are adding numbers with opposite signs, you subtract the absolute values of the two numbers and assign the sign of the number with the greatest absolute value." What a difference in student learning between this class where different models and visualization are standard operating procedure and one in which they are not.

No wonder math scores in this reasonably diverse and typically middle-class K–8 school were going up. It wasn't fancy new programs or contorted interventions that were making the difference. Rather it was *coaching, collaboration, and a culture of professional growth*, all focusing on strengthening the quality of daily math instruction, that explained the quality I observed.

We've known for years that people can't do what they can't envision. People won't do what they don't understand. People can't do well what isn't practiced, and practice without feedback results in little change. And unless these processes are done collaboratively, little is sustained or institutionalized. Thus, the key to raising the quality of day-in-and-day-out classroom mathematics instruction is a systematic focus on helping teachers of mathematics envision, understand, practice, receive feedback, and collaborate—an agenda requiring knowledgeable, well-trained, and respected *Mathematics Teacher Leader Coaches (Math TLCs)*.

A Plea to Recruit, Deploy, Train, Support, and Honor Cadres of Math Teacher Leader Coaches

In the post-Sputnik era, the nation's schools were populated with NSF institute graduates who became recognized as math and science leaders. In the 1990s the math field benefited greatly from Woodrow Wilson Fellows, and Texas Instruments' supported Teachers Teaching with Technology. These relatively small initiatives served as launching pads for two generations of K–12 school mathematics leaders, and many have gone on to win Presidential Awards for Excellence in Teaching Mathematics and other recognitions. Sadly, there are no equivalent programs or opportunities today.

Consider other arenas where coaching is the norm. Despite million-dollar player salaries, the New York Yankees have a twenty-six-person roster, one manager, and seven coaches. The Washington Redskins have a fifty-three-person roster and twenty coaches and trainers. The Los Angeles Lakers have a twelve-person roster and four coaches. The typical 500-student school has twenty teachers, one overworked principal, and rarely any coaches. Is it any surprise that so many innovations are short-term in their impact and that so little really changes in the nation's classrooms?

Consider then the potential impact of, for example, the Intel Math TLCs or the Broad Foundation Math TLCs. Envision a partnership between a corporation or foundation, a school district, and a college or university that collaboratively recruits, selects, trains, deploys, and honors a cadre of Math TLCs. At $90,000 per Math TLC for eleven months (including a two-week summer institute), $3 million would provide the salary for thirty Teacher Leader Coaches and leave $300,000 for training, support, recognition, and program administration, with the assumption that the school district would assume the costs of all benefits. Thirty Teacher Leader Coaches, each deployed to one school for four days per week, or to two schools for two days each per week, leaving Fridays for training, would provide direct service and stimulus to between thirty and sixty schools, depending upon size and need.

Moving Forward

To help move this timely and critical idea forward, a draft job description and some potential recruitment, deployment, training, and recognition approaches follow.

Draft Job Description

General Expectations

The position of Mathematics TLC (Math TLC) is designed to provide a diverse array of services and activities that (1) guide the improvement of the quality of mathematics instruction within a school, (2) support the effective implementation of the letter and the spirit of the Common Core State Standards for Mathematics, and (3) orchestrate a range of professional learning community activities for the school's teachers of mathematics. Accordingly, the job of Math TLC is likely to include, but not necessarily be limited to the following:

- providing expert guidance and direction
- providing support and flak interference
- acting as co-planner, co-teacher, and/or co-assessor, hand-in-hand with colleagues
- modeling effective instructional practices
- serving as observer, and subsequently, as provider of positive and negative critique of practice
- promoting, organizing, and supporting professional interaction among teachers

Math TLCs are supervised by the building principal or his/her designee, are evaluated by district's mathematics or curriculum leadership personnel, and serve at the pleasure of the school's teachers of mathematics on the basis on annual positive votes to retain by a minimum of two-thirds of these teachers.

Specific Responsibilities

In the domain of *curriculum*, the Math TLC will be expected to actively support the implementation of a coherent mathematics curriculum throughout the school, including grade-level content and process expectations, appropriate print and electronic instructional materials, and a viable pacing guide. Among the specific responsibilities in this domain are the following:

- helping every teacher of mathematics understand the big ideas and the mathematical processes of the grade-level curriculum
- helping every teacher of mathematics understand the mathematics contained within the content expectations
- helping every teacher of mathematics make effective use of available instructional materials and resources

In the domain of *instruction*, the Math TLC will be expected to lead the adoption or adaptation of a common vision of effective teaching of mathematics and support the planning for, implementation of, and reflection upon the elements of this vision. Among the specific responsibilities in this domain are the following:

- co-planning and co-teaching mathematics lessons and collaboratively reflecting upon and debriefing the experience with a focus on what can be improved and how to make these improvement
- observing instruction with a focus on the elements of the common vision of effective teaching and providing oral and written feedback with specific suggestions for improvement

In the domain of *assessment*, the Math TLC will be expected to ensure that a set of aligned formative, benchmark, and summative assessments are in place and used to monitor student, teacher, and school accomplishment at the unit/chapter and grade/course levels. Among the specific responsibilities in this domain are the following:

- assisting every teacher of mathematics to create high-quality assessments of mathematical skills, concepts, and applications
- assisting every teacher of mathematics to interpret student, class, and school assessment data and use these analyses to devise plans of action
- helping teachers analyze student work to monitor needs and successes

In the domain of *professional development*, the Math TLC will be expected to plan and coordinate the implementation of an ongoing set of experiences that support professional growth within a culture of dignity, transparency, collaboration, and support. Among the specific responsibilities in this domain are the following:

- coaching teachers on the effectiveness of classroom instruction, including identifying the degree to which there was opportunity to learn, evidence of that learning or lack of learning, elements of the lesson that worked and why they worked, elements of the lesson that did not work and why, missed opportunities, and a plan for improvement
- planning, orchestrating, implementing, and evaluating professional learning community experiences among all, or a subset, of the teachers of mathematics in the school, including lesson analysis, task analysis, video analysis, student work analysis, data analysis, and common readings about curriculum instruction and the implications of research findings; effective teachers rely on relevant contexts to engage their students' interest and use questions to stimulate thinking and to create language-rich mathematics classrooms

In the domain of *mathematics program leadership*, the Math TLC will be expected to provide leadership in securing the resources and support needed to implement an effective mathematics program. Among the specific responsibilities in this domain are the following:

- advocating for all necessary resources, policies, and support to meet the goal of high levels of mathematics achievement by all students
- collaborating with other Math TLCs and mentoring teachers to become Math TLCs
- representing teachers' needs and concerns to school and district administrators
- modeling and motivating professional growth, collaboration, and excellence

Qualifications

- a minimum of five years of successful K–12 teaching experience in mathematics
- a familiarity with elements of effective mathematics instruction, elements of effective professional learning communities, and the Common Core State Standards for Mathematics

- a record of working effectively with colleagues
- a passion for improving the quality of instruction through collaborative work with teachers
- an eagerness to learn more about how to support high levels of student achievement in mathematics

Potential Approaches to Recruit, Deploy, Train, and Recognize Math TLCs

Recruiting and Selecting

- high-quality brochure and accompanying website
- reasonable application process (so as not to serve as a disincentive) that focuses on the qualifications and employs an interview to validate the written application

Deploying

- identify neediest schools *with potential* (deploying a Math TLC to a dysfunctional school serves no purpose as the school infrastructure and culture are unlikely to be ready to benefit from the services of a Math TLC)
- usually not deployed to a school in which the Math TLC has been a teacher
- deployed for one year, with the expectation of redeployment at the same school subject to a two-thirds or more vote to retain by the teachers of mathematics

Training

- Every Friday, the cadre of Math TLCs gathers for a three-part, all-day agenda
  - common learning experience to expand Math TLC knowledge base, based on needs assessment
  - structured sharing about highs and lows, successes and failures, and challenges faced
  - professional learning community activity orchestrated by selected Math TLCs
- The cadre of Math TLCs gathers for a two-week institute each summer with a focus, as appropriate, on the following:
  - mathematics content
  - mathematics instructional practices
  - coaching techniques

- building effective professional learning communities
- providing leadership

Recognition

- annual dinner celebrations to thank and honor accomplishments
- financial support to cover expenses for attending conferences, workshops, and seminars

Coordination and Administration

- Depending on situation and circumstances, the Math TLC program can be run out of the school district office, an intermediate unit, or partnering college or university, but, at a minimum, a part-time coordinator/administrator is a necessity.

CHANGING THE SYSTEM

Tidy Events and Messy Processes

I find it interesting that the more often we invoke the mantra "change is a process, not an event," the more we seem to honor events as primary indicators of change.

Just think of how we answer the question "What's new?" We talk about our new curriculum or our new textbook. We speak about our new three-year mathematics graduation requirement—including algebra—or our new block schedule. We respond that we've got two new classroom sets of TI-83s or that we've just finished a two-week summer workshop on the effective use of manipulatives. These are all obviously worthy of pride, but they all also tend to represent top-down, product-oriented, voted-in *events* that have only marginal impact on the overall system and that rarely result in substantive improvement.

Now think of how rarely "What's new?" is greeted by the far fuzzier—but far more influential—changes in process. For example, we hail the new materials we've adopted but rarely acclaim the revisions to the materials-selection process that are more important than ever. We recognize staff development events but rarely focus on the long-term process of educating principals, superintendents, and members of boards of education who are so crucial for the success of mathematics reform. And we still focus enormous time and energy on producing curriculum guides and frameworks that few bother to read, let alone use, when devoting a fraction of this time to assuring that our assessments were aligned with the curriculum would pay far richer systemic dividends.

But none of this should be surprising. It's easy to mandate such things as time requirements, curriculum guidelines, professional development sessions, and new materials. That is, it is easy to create an infrastructure from the top down. It's an entirely different matter getting the infrastructure to work and changing beliefs, behaviors, and practices. This is where we need to facilitate, where we need processes, where change is bottom-up, and where our collective attention needs to be focused.

Accordingly, we must shift our thinking from the tidy planning and implementation of events to the messy establishment of ongoing processes that reform the system. We need to ask ourselves the following questions:

- What ongoing processes do we have in place to shift beliefs about mathematics and teaching mathematics?

- What ongoing processes do we have in place to significantly increase professional interaction?

- What ongoing processes do we have in place to enlist the active support of principals, superintendents, and members of boards of education?

- What ongoing processes do we have in place to engender stronger public support for high-quality mathematics education?

Nowhere in all the volumes of data and commentary on the recently released Third International Mathematics and Science Study (TIMSS) has this notion of a need to shift our attention from creating an infrastructure to *making the infrastructure work* been clearer than in the comparison of pedagogical approaches used in Germany, Japan, and the United States. After making a rather compelling case that the similarities in terms of curriculum, time, teachers, and students are far greater than the differences, TIMSS (*Pursuing Excellence*, pages 42–44) presents stark differences in terms of typical eighth-grade mathematics lessons. While the typical Japanese lesson parallels the vision of our Standards and focuses on understanding, the typical United States lesson emphasized skill acquisition (see Figure 3–6 on page 32). The extensive videotape study also found that while over three-quarters of the grade-eight topics were developed conceptually in Germany and Japan, only one-quarter of these topics were developed conceptually in the United States. Alternatively, over three-quarters of the topics taught in the United States were presented in the relatively passive "teachers prescribe, students transcribe" mode with little attention to conceptual understanding (see Figure A–1).

What should be clear is that changing these classroom practices requires much more than the top-down events that merely build an infrastructure. Thanks to TIMSS, we know better than ever what problems we face. Thanks to the growing body of research on systemic reform, we have better answers than ever to solving these problems. All that's left is rolling up our sleeves and implementing the messy and varied processes that foster genuine systemic reform and improved student achievement. It's a challenge I believe we are up to.

Figure A–1 *Average percentage of topinc in eighth-grade mathematics lessons that are stated or developed*

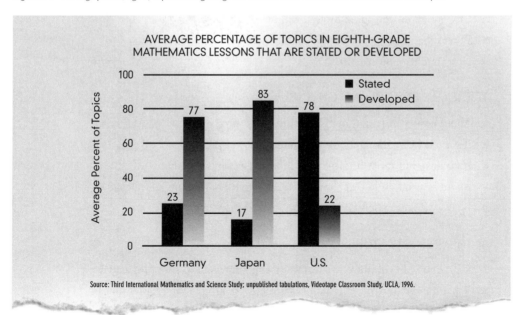

Source: Third International Mathematics and Science Study; unpublished tabulations, Videotape Classroom Study, UCLA, 1996.

This article first appeared in the January 1997 NCSM *Newsletter*.

MAKING MATH COMMONPLACE AND REAL FOR OUR CHILDREN

Some thoughts to share with parents from Steve Leinwand

Parents can best support the mathematical development of their children by making mathematics commonplace and fun whenever and wherever it occurs naturally in our daily lives. Questions can be simple and informal, and answers can be responded to with "How did you get that?" or "Share with us your thinking?" For example:

AT MCDONALD'S OR ANY OTHER FAST FOOD RESTAURANT—IN LINE OR AT THE DRIVE-THROUGH:

- How much do you think your order will cost?
- What's the least and most expensive reasonable meal we could order?
- Can we all get a meal and spend less than $20? How?
- About how much should the tax be?
- Is a Happy Meal a good deal?
- Does it make sense to order large soda if there are free refills?

AT THE RESTAURANT:

- You can spend up to $8 without going over. What could you order?
- How much do you think the bill will be?
- What's the most expensive reasonable meal we could order?
- How much should we tip?

AT THE GAS STATION AND ON A TRIP:

- About how many miles per gallon are we getting?
- If gas is $4.09/gallon, about how much will we spend?
- If we have only $30, how many gallons of gas can we get?
- About how much longer should it take us to there (looking at mileage signs)?
- If it's 1:30 now, when do you think we'll get there?

AT THE GROCERY STORE:

- How much do you think we just spent (looking at a full shopping cart)?
- What fractional part of the items is taxable (looking at the register tape)?
- About how much do we pay per item in the cart?

- What should the scale say if we order 1½ pounds of cheese?
- About how much will three-quarters of a pound of ham cost?
- What's the unit price? Which is the best buy?
- What does it say on the nutrition label?

AT THE BANK:

- What's a withdrawal? What's a deposit? Which is addition and which is subtraction?
- If I have $_____, how much will I have after a deposit/withdraw of $_____?

IN THE KITCHEN:

- Recipes (Can you measure that much out? How much more or less? Suppose we doubled/halved the recipe?)
- Measuring cups and spoons
- Ounces, cups, pints, quarts and gallons, ounces and pounds

FROM THE NEWSPAPER:

- Graphs and tables
- Sports statistics
- Scavenger hunts (for percents, for numbers greater than 1000, etc.)

JUST FOR FUN ANYTIME:

- About how big is that? (height, width, weight, capacity)
- About how many would fit? (For example: How many dogs could fit in the car? How many McNuggets boxes could fit in the trunk? About how many people could fit in this room?)

POWERFUL GAMES:

- Yahtzee
- Cribbage
- Card games

GIVING STUDENTS THE BENEFIT OF THE DOUBT

It used to be so much easier. Doing mathematics meant getting right answers. Whether it was a straightforward exercise or a more involved problem, the choice was almost always between right and wrong—between a black check and a red "X." If right: Great! Full credit. If wrong: Tough! No credit. Correctness and accuracy were all that counted, and grades were easily computed by aggregating the checks or subtracting the Xs from 100. Mathematics was the paragon of objectivity, and we rarely had to worry about giving students the benefit of the doubt because in the dichotomous world of right and wrong, there was simply no doubt.

But then came the expanded focus on solving problems and communicating mathematically. Along came accessible and inexpensive calculators that provided speed as well as accuracy. And with these changes we've had to deal with a growing recognition that authentic work and the demonstration of understanding are increasingly even more important than a page of right answers.

Very quickly these changes have made things very messy. We've been forced to enter the world of partial credit, holistic scoring, and rubrics. We've had to shift toward more subjective scoring schemas. And we've come to recognize the need to more frequently give our students the benefit of the doubt.

These issues recently became much clearer to me when we holistically scored the open-ended items on the tenth-grade Connecticut Academic Performance Test (CAPT). We established a general policy that judgment calls were nearly always resolved by pausing and thinking about which score gave the student the benefit of the doubt. That is, did the response show sufficient evidence of understanding, even if the correct answer was missing?

We built the scoring system around the following four-point generic rubric or scoring guide:

A score of 3 reflects *full and complete* understanding of all concepts and processes embodied in the problem. It means that the task was addressed in a mathematically sound manner and that the response may contain minor arithmetic errors

A score of 2 reflects *reasonable*, although incomplete, understanding of the essential concepts and processes embodied in the problem. It means that the response contains most of the attributes of an appropriate response. However, the flaws it contains do not offset countervailing evidence that the student understands the essential mathematical ideas addressed by the task.

A score of 1 reflects *limited* understanding of some of the concepts and processes embodied in the problem. It means that the response contains only some of the attributes of an appropriate response and that the flaws it contains provide evidence of insufficient understanding and knowledge of the ideas addressed by the task.

A score of 0 reflects *merely an acquaintance* with the topic. It means that the response contains few or none of the attributes of an appropriate response and that there is little or no evidence of understanding of the ideas addressed by the task.

Our hope is that the use of this generic rubric on the CAPT test will encourage its widespread use on a much larger scale in classrooms across the state. Our hope is that educators will experiment with such four-point scoring scales as they move away from the traditional—albeit limiting—100-point scale with which we are so familiar. And our hope is that parents and students will come to appreciate that a 3 out of 4 holistic score tied to clearly articulated rubrics and samples of student work is a much more meaningful measure of accomplishment than a grade of 80 on an always changing scale of 100.

So welcome to the exciting world of increased ambiguity, more subjectivity, and harder-to-make judgments that characterize assessments of mathematical power. It sure used to be a lot easier, but that was when life was a lot simpler and mathematics was a lot narrower.

This article first appeared in the *ATOMIC Journal*, Spring 1995.

CHARACTERISTICS OF EXCELLENCE

How Does Your School Measure Up?

Created for the American Productivity and Quality Council's Mathematics and Science Benchmarking Project

4 DOMAINS:	18 COMPONENTS:
Vision, Planning, and Leadership	Vision Strategic Planning Designated Leadership Data-driven Decision Making Program Evaluation
Core Programmatic Elements	Curriculum Standards Instructional Materials Instructional Practices Assessment
Personnel and Professional Development	Recruitment, Hiring, and Induction Professional Interaction and Sharing Professional Development Supervision and Evaluation
Programmatic Support	Community Support Intervention and Remedial Assistance Adequate Resources Expectations and Accountability A Culture of Productive Professionalism

DOMAINS	COMPONENTS	CHARACTERISTICS
Vision, Planning, and Leadership	Vision	**1.** A written vision of high-quality teaching and learning of mathematics and science has been developed.
		2. The vision is based on research findings in the fields of mathematics education and cognitive psychology.
		3. A broad set of stakeholders were involved in developing the vision.
		4. The vision is published, widely available, and frequently referred to.
	Strategic Planning	**1.** A strategic plan for the ongoing improvement of student achievement in mathematics and science exists.
		2. The strategic plan contains specific and measureable goals and objectives.
		3. The strategic plan is updated annually.
		4. A broad set of stakeholders has input into the strategic plan.
	Designated Leadership	**1.** One or more mathematics program leaders have been designated.
		2. Program leaders provide direction and coordination in the areas of curriculum design, instructional materials, assessment, and professional development and ensure the alignment of effort.
		3. Program leaders use a variety of strategies to communicate with diverse stakeholders about the goals and objectives of the program.
		4. Program leaders forge partnerships to support the vision and goals of the program.
		5. There is a sense of urgency and high expectations for accomplishment that pervade the system.
	Data-driven Decision Making	**1.** A comprehensive system exists for collecting, organizing, accessing, reporting, and sharing a wide range of data about the program.
		2. Existing policies and program activities are periodically reviewed and rejustified based on data.
		3. New policies and practices are developed and evaluated on the basis of data.
		4. Data is regularly disaggregated—by school, region, teacher, ethnicity, and so on—to make finer distinctions.
		5. Teachers and administrators are adept at data analysis and the translation of data into actions.

DOMAINS	COMPONENTS	CHARACTERISTICS
Vision, Planning, and Leadership *(continued)*	Program Evaluation	**1.** Course and grade-level review and improvement committees exist to make annual recommendations for change and improvement and to oversee the implementation of these recommendations.
		2. Annual program reviews are conducted, including landscape scans of student achievement, enrollment trends, apparent strengths and weaknesses, and an action plan.
		3. Five-year program audits are conducted, including internal analysis and external review of all aspects of the program, and result in detailed plans for improvement.
		4. Multiple sets of data about the program are gathered over time, shared with stakeholders, and used to analyze the effectiveness of all aspects of the program.
		5. Gap analysis and a focus on narrowing gaps is a key aspect of program evaluation.
Core Programmatic Elements	Curriculum Standards	**1.** A coherent set of districtwide grade-level and course expectations has been developed to guide the instructional program.
		2. The standards and expectations have been developed collaboratively by teachers responsible for their implementation.
		3. There are no more than thirty-five grade-level expectations per grade or course.
		4. There is a clear sense of the "big ideas" that become focal points for each grade or course.
		5. There is the expectation of mastery and a reduction of repetition of previously taught material.
		6. There is a balance among the standards of procedural knowledge, conceptual understanding, and application/ problem solving.
		7. There are expectations for interdisciplinary study within the curriculum.
		8. The curriculum standards and expectations are aligned with the vision.
		9. The features and changes in the curriculum, and their implications, are communicated and justified to all stakeholders.

DOMAINS	COMPONENTS	CHARACTERISTICS
Core Programmatic Elements *(continued)*	Instructional Materials	**1.** A wide variety of print and nonprint instructional materials are available to every teacher to support the implementation of the curricular expectations. **2.** The curriculum provides suggestions on how best to use and incorporate instructional materials to meet the curricular expectations. **3.** An adequate supply of textbooks and other supplemental print resources is readily available within each school. **4.** An adequate supply of concrete materials including science kits, manipulative materials, and laboratory equipment is available and regularly replenished. **5.** An adequate supply of calculators, computers, software, LCD projectors, probes, smart boards, and other electronic technology is available and regularly used.
	Instructional Practices	**1.** It is consistently evident that lessons have been carefully planned and that the focus of each lesson is drawn from the grade or course expectations. **2.** A clear balance among skills, concepts, and applications is evident in typical instruction. **3.** In addition to skills and concepts, instruction consistently addresses problem solving, reasoning, and inquiry. **4.** Alternative approaches and multiple representations are consistently employed to reach more students. **5.** Context and connections are used to engage learners.

DOMAINS	COMPONENTS	CHARACTERISTICS
Core Programmatic Elements *(continued)*	Assessment	**1.** A system of district-level formative and summative assessments is in place for each grade and each course.
		2. The assessments are carefully aligned with the curricular expectations and measure what matters.
		3. Formative assessments are used to adjust instruction, guide reteaching and other interventions, and monitor short-term mastery of content.
		4. Summative assessments for each grade and each course are used to monitor the success of instruction, guide revisions and improvements, and assess student mastery of core content.
		5. All formative and summative assessments are collaboratively developed.
		6. The data from formative and summative assessments is readily available to teachers and other appropriate educators.
		7. There is a balance of item types (short answer, extended response, essay, etc.) on all assessments.
		8. Multiple measures of achievement, such as portfolios, student work, observations, are used to assess student progress and program quality.
		9. All formative and summative assessments are reviewed annually and revised as necessary.

DOMAINS	COMPONENTS	CHARACTERISTICS
Personnel and Professional Development	Recruitment, Hiring, and Induction	**1.** The district or school uses a broad net for recruiting the most qualified prospective teachers. **2.** The hiring process includes interviews and demonstration teaching. **3.** A two-year comprehensive induction program exists for all beginning teachers with mentors, special opportunities to observe colleagues, and intensive supervision. **4.** The result of the recruitment, hiring, and induction processes is a relatively low turnover rate among teachers.
	Professional Interaction and Sharing	**1.** Policies and strategies are in place to create ongoing professional learning communities among teachers. **2.** Principals and other administrators support and encourage ongoing professional interaction. **3.** Teachers are provided structured time to collaborate. **4.** Opportunities exist for teachers to collaboratively plan lessons, observe each other teaching, analyze videos of lessons, and analyze student work. **5.** Teachers use common readings and collegial seminars to initiate shared discussions.
	Professional Development	**1.** Each teacher has an individual professional development plan. **2.** Collaborative professional development is collegially planned and aligned with specific programmatic needs. **3.** Professional development is provided to support the effective use of instructional materials—print, concrete, and electronic. **4.** The focus of all professional development is a balance between mathematics or science content knowledge and pedagogical content knowledge. **5.** A cadre of trained instructional coaches is available to support high-quality teaching. **6.** Opportunities to attend conferences and seminars exist.
	Supervision and Evaluation	**1.** Teachers are regularly observed, in person or on video, and coached about ways of improving practice and impact. **2.** Teacher evaluation is conducted by knowledgeable evaluators, using a collaboratively developed evaluation protocol that focuses on the planning, implementation, and assessment of instruction.

DOMAINS	COMPONENTS	CHARACTERISTICS
Programmatic Support	Community Support	**1.** High-quality partnerships are established with higher education institutions and with the business and industrial communities.
		2. Parents are viewed as essential partners and are made to feel welcome in their children's school and are encouraged to contact teachers and administrators.
		3. Regular parent nights are conducted to keep parents abreast of the key aspects of the school's instructional program.
		4. Extensive use of volunteer assistance is made throughout the system.
		5. The district and schools develop clear messages about their mathematics and science programs and disseminate these messages widely.
	Intervention and Remedial Assistance	**1.** Additional, supplemental programming is available to every student who demonstrates the need for such assistance.
		2. All intervention and supplemental or remedial programs are conducted at times in addition to regular instruction and are aligned with the curricular expectations of regular instruction.
		3. All intervention and supplemental instruction is conducted by trained and knowledgeable teachers or tutors capable of maximizing the impact of such programs.
	Adequate Resources	**1.** Adequate allocations of time during the school day are devoted to mathematics and science instruction.
		2. Adequate budgetary allocations are made to ensure sufficient staffing, materials, and professional development.
	Expectations and Accountability	**1.** Clear high expectations—for students and adults—are set, communicated, and widely modeled in word and deed.
		2. Every adult is aware of the expectations for professional behavior and held accountable for meeting these expectations.
	A Culture of Productive Professionalism	**1.** There is a tangible and non-negotiable commitment to continuous improvement.
		2. Teachers are treated as professionals and students are treated with dignity.
		3. Every adult in the system believes and acts on the belief that all students can learn.

LEARNING MORE ABOUT SCHOOL MATHEMATICS AND THE COMMON CORE STATE STANDARDS FOR MATHEMATICS

The ten resources listed below represent the places I am most likely to turn to for ideas, news, and inspiration about doing my job better.

About School Mathematics

1. *Adding It Up: Helping Children Learn Mathematics*. National Research Council, National Academy Press, Washington, DC, 2001. Available for free download at: www.nap.edu/catalog.php?record_id=9822

    This clearly written and compelling book provides the research base for effective teaching and learning of school mathematics.

2. *Principles and Standards for School Mathematics*. National Council of Teachers of Mathematics, Reston, VA, 2000.

    This updated and consolidated version of the original "NCTM Standards" provides a wealth of guidance, direction, and examples.

3. Inside Mathematics: A Professional Resource for Educations. See www.insidemathematics.org

    This site features classroom examples of innovative teaching methods and insights into student learning, tools for mathematics instruction that teachers can use immediately, and video tours of the ideas and materials on the site.

4. *Accessible Mathematics: 10 Instructional Shifts That Raise Student Achievement*. Steven Leinwand, Heinemann, 2009.

    The author of *Sensible Mathematics* describes a set of powerful, research-affirmed, and easy-to-adapt instructional strategies for mathematics.

About the Common Core State Standards for Mathematics

5. The Common Core State Standards for Mathematics. 2010. Available at www.corestandards.org/the-standards

    This is the homepage for the Common Core State Standards.

6. The Partnership for Assessment and Readiness for College and Careers. See http://parcconline.org

    This is the homepage for one of the two CCSS assessment consortia.

7. The Smarter Balanced Assessment Consortium. See www.smarterbalanced.org

    This is the homepage for the other CCSS assessment consortium.

8. Tools for the Common Core Standards. See http://commoncoretools.wordpress.com

    This is the website/blog that CCSSM writer Bill McCallum uses to post resources and updates.

About Leadership for School Mathematics

9. *The PRIME Leadership Framework.* National Council of Supervisors of Mathematics. Denver, CO. 2008. See www.ncsmonline.org

    This resource defines and describes a set of leadership principles, indicators, and actions that frame the expectations for effective mathematics education leaders.

10. *Standards for Professional Learning.* Learning Forward. Available at www.learningforward.org/standards/index.cfm

    There are the research-based standards for professional development that should inform all decisions about professional development.

Additional Works Cited

Everybody Counts: A Report to the Nation on the Future of Mathematics Education, National Research Council, National Academy Press, Washington, DC, 1989.

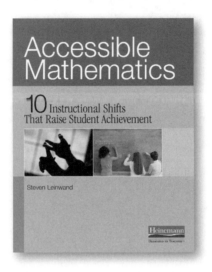